Language, History, and Metanarrative in the Fiction of Julian Barnes

Studies in Twentieth-Century British Literature

Karen Marguerite Radell
General Editor

Vol. 3

PETER LANG
New York • Washington, D.C./Baltimore • Bern
Frankfurt am Main • Berlin • Brussels • Vienna • Oxford

Bruce Sesto

Language, History, and Metanarrative in the Fiction of Julian Barnes

PETER LANG
New York • Washington, D.C./Baltimore • Bern
Frankfurt am Main • Berlin • Brussels • Vienna • Oxford

Library of Congress Cataloging-in-Publication Data

Sesto, Bruce.
Language, history, and metanarrative in the fiction of Julian Barnes / Bruce Sesto.
p. cm. — (Studies in twentieth-century British literature; vol. 3)
Includes bibliographical references.
1. Barnes, Julian—History and criticism. 2. Literature and history—
England—History—20th century. 3. Experimental fiction,
English—History and criticism. 4. Postmodernism (Literature)—
England. 5. Narration (Rhetoric). I. Title. II. Series.
PR6052.A6657Z87   823'.914—dc21   99-24975
ISBN 0-8204-4467-7
ISSN 1091-8574

Die Deutsche Bibliothek-CIP-Einheitsaufnahme

Sesto, Bruce:
Language, history, and metanarrative in the fiction of Julian Barnes / Bruce Sesto.
–New York; Washington, D.C./Baltimore; Bern;
Frankfurt am Main; Berlin; Brussels; Vienna; Oxford: Lang.
(Studies in twentieth-century British literature; Vol. 3)
ISBN 0-8204-4467-7

The paper in this book meets the guidelines for permanence and durability
of the Committee on Production Guidelines for Book Longevity
of the Council of Library Resources.

© 2001 Peter Lang Publishing, Inc., New York

All rights reserved.
Reprint or reproduction, even partially, in all forms such as microfilm,
xerography, microfiche, microcard, and offset strictly prohibited.

Printed in the United States of America

Contents

Introduction	Julian Barnes and Postmodernist Fiction	1
Chapter 1	Youth and Marriage	13
Chapter 2	*Flaubert's Parrot*	31
Chapter 3	*A History of the World in 10 1/2 Chapters*	53
Chapter 4	*The Porcupine*	113
Bibliography		129

Introduction

Julian Barnes and Postmodernist Fiction

In his introduction to *Newwriting*, an anthology of contemporary English fiction and poetry, British critic and novelist Malcom Bradbury numbers Julian Barnes among the new generation of British writers "who no longer [feel] bound to realism, and who freely [explore] surrealism, fantasy, and metafictional play" (6). By "realism" Bradbury is referring, of course, to the narrative and rhetorical conventions which came to dominate British fiction from the mid-nineteenth to the early twentieth century (culminating in the works of George Eliot, Arnold Bennett, and John Galsworthy), and which, after being eclipsed by the modernist aestheticism of the 1910s and 20s, re-surfaced in the novels of George Orwell, Christopher Isherwood, and Evelyn Waugh, and then again, nearly a generation later, in the prose fictions of Philip Larkin, Kingsley Amis, and John Wain.

Notwithstanding individual variations in technique, all realist writers seem to share the notion that language is a transparent medium of representation, and that "reality," owing to this special capacity of language, can be faith- fully transcribed in fiction. According to David Lodge, "realism" refers not only to the "mimetic representation of experience," but also to the "organization of narrative according to a logic of causality and temporal sequence" (*Newwriting* 205). As Lodge goes on to explain, however, the structuralists and their "descendants" regard realism as "an art of bad faith because it seeks to disguise or deny its own conventionality" (*After Bakhtin* 13). The writers of Barnes' generation problematize realist conventions by using an array of metafictional narrative strategies—including authorial intrusion, framing structures, and intertextual parody—to expose the fictionality of literary representation. This is not to argue, however, that postmodern metafictional texts reject the "real world." Rather they redefine, or reformulate, that world by first installing and then subverting the conventions of literary realism. As Lodge argues, "it would be false to oppose metafiction to realism; rather metafiction makes explicit the implicit problematic of realism" (*After Bakhtin* 19).

The immediate effect of postmodernism's impulse to reveal the artifice of fiction has been to undermine literary art's once vaunted status as repository and transmitter of universal truth. As Alison Lee observes in *Realism and Power: Postmodern British Fiction*, "Literature, because constructed in language, is not a privileged form of discourse, and therefore has no special claims as an emissary of 'truth'" (59). Similarly, Linda Hutcheon, who stresses postmodernism's adversarial relationship to liberal humanism, argues that contemporary theory's insistent emphasis on contextualization has resulted in the dethroning of one of humanism's most cherished values—the idea of timeless truth. To Hutcheon, "Postmodern works . . . contest art's right to claim to inscribe timeless universal values, and they do so by thematizing and even formally enacting the context-dependent nature of all values" (*A Poetics of Postmodernism* 90).

Not surprisingly, perhaps, it was the modernists who (after some initial coaxing from their "Symbolist" forbears) spearheaded the revolt against 19th century realism. According to Lodge:

> . . . Modernism turned its back on the traditional idea of art as imitation of life and substituted the idea of art as an autonomous activity. The fundamental principle of aesthetics before the modern era was that art imitates life, and is therefore in the last analysis answerable to it: art must tell the truth about life. (*After Bakhtin* 5)

To modernists like Henry James, Joseph Conrad, James Joyce and Virginia Woolf, "the truth about life" resided not in external reality but rather in individual consciousness:

> . . . modernist novelists sought radical redefinitions of the real. One such redefinition is based on the view that, since the individual always perceives reality through his or her own consciousness, the contents and structure of consciousness represent the only accessible reality. (Wynne-Davies, 114).

This solipsistic view of reality gave rise to an era of unprecedented literary innovation. Since reality was ultimately a matter of subjective experience, new forms of fiction had to be created in order to render the labyrinthine intricacies of mental perception. Novelists began to experiment with point-of-view and narrative chronology. These developments, coupled with the increasingly self-conscious use of language and figurative patterns, suggested that the modernists placed higher priority on the idea of the literary work as an autonomous verbal structure than as an accurate reflector of empirical reality. As Marguerite Alexander observes:

> A foregrounding of language is among the principal characteristics of modernism. Modernists worked on the principle that language elicits a direct response from the reader, independently of meaning. Moreover, their work, at its most characteristic, is self-referential, generating meaning only as the parts relate to the whole, rather than through an implied reference to the everyday world. The aesthetic of modernism demanded that the text be seen as an impersonal artefact, comparable to other art forms. (6)

As the preceding passage suggests, modernist and postmodernist fictions share certain characteristics. Like their modernist precursors, for instance, postmodernist texts challenge the central tenets of literary realism, particularly those which center on definitions of "reality" and the problem of artistic representation. Furthermore, both traditions' respective assaults on realist conventions necessitated the invention of new forms of literary expression—a rage for experimentation which manifested itself, in each case, in a heightening of linguistic and narrative self-consciousness.

However, it is the debate over precisely where the modernist and postmodernist "traditions" diverge (or if indeed they do diverge) which has become one of the central preoccupations of contemporary criticism. To many critics, including Robert Alter, Brian McHale, and Alan Wilde, the most crucial difference between modernist and postmodernist fiction is the latter's overtly self-conscious delineation of the "ontological" aspects of literary representation. Robert Stam elucidates the nature of this problem in *Reflexivity in Film and Literature:*

> All art has been nourished by the perennial tension between illusionism and reflexivity. All artistic representation can pass itself off as 'reality' or straightforwardly admit its status as representation. Illusionism pretends to be something more than mere artistic production; it presents its characters as real people, its sequence of words or images as real time, and its representations as substantiated fact. Reflexivity, on the other hand, points to its own mask and invites the public to examine its design and texture. Reflexive works break with art as enchantment and call attention to their own factitiousness as textual constructs. (1)

Stam further argues that

> While illusionist art strives for an impression of spatio-temporal coherence, anti-illusionist art calls attention to the gaps and holes and seams in the narrative

tissue. To the suave continuities of illusionism, it opposes the shocks of rupture and discontinuity. (7)

Whereas the modernist's quest for textual impersonality precluded such techniques as authorial intrusion, postmodernist authors frequently insert themselves into their texts in order to expose ontological "seams" and thereby reveal the inherent "constructedness" of fictional works. As David Lodge observes:

> I cannot think offhand of any instance in the work of James, Conrad, Woolf and Joyce (up to and including *Ulysses*) where the fictitiousness of the narrative is exposed as blatantly as in my last few examples [Vonnegut's *Slaughterhouse Five* and Joseph Heller's *Good As Gold*]. The reason, I believe, is that such exposure foregrounds the existence of the author, the source of the novel's diegesis, in a way which ran counter to the modernist pursuit of impersonality and mimesis of consciousness. (*After Bakhtin* 43)

To Lodge, who argues that it is the contemporary writer's preference for diegesis over mimesis which, in part, distinguishes postmodernist from modernist fiction, authorial intrusion as a narrative device has never been so widespread, a phenomenon which he views as paradoxical in light of poststructuralism's assault on the "author" via Barthes and Foucault:

> The foregrounding of the act of authorship within the boundaries of the text which is such a common feature of contemporary fiction, is a defensive response, either conscious or intuitive, to the questioning of the idea of the author and of the mimetic function of fiction by modern critical theory. (*After Bakhtin* 19)

Similarly, in *Partial Magic*, Robert Alter distinguishes between the "artful" novel (modernist) and the novel which calls attention to its own artifice (postmodernist):

> I should like to make clear that a self-conscious novel, where the artifice is deliberately exposed, is by no means identical with an elaborately artful novel, where the artifice may perhaps be prominent. The first-person narrators, for example, of Conrad's *Lord Jim* and Ford Madox Ford's *The Good Soldier*, on some level make us aware of the intricate artifice of their narrations as they circle round and round the same central events, gradually divulging more and more information, leading us to experience through the narrative pattern itself the complexity and elusiveness of morally judging people and their actions. Nevertheless, in both those novels the conspicuous elaboration of narrative artifice is performed in the service of a moral and psychological realism, operating even in its occasional improbabilities as a technique of verisimilitude, not as a testing ground of the ontological status of the fiction. Conrad and Ford give us the world through a labyrinthine narrative because that seems to them the most faithful way of representing a labyrinthine world. (*xiii*)

By contrast, Alter maintains, a truly self-conscious novel is one in which "there is a consistent effort to convey to us a sense of the fictional world as an authorial construct set up against a background of literary tradition and convention" (xi).

Implicit in Alter's statements is a thesis which Brian McHale develops more fully in his book *Postmodernist Fiction*. For McHale the modernist poetic is one which employs linguistic and narrative resources in the pursuit of epistemological verification. Typically organized around questions concerning the ways in which we interpret reality, the modernist text deploys multiple narrators, retrospective narration, limited point-of-view, and interior monologue in order to explore the nature of human understanding. Thus, according to McHale, paradigmatic modernist texts like *Heart of Darkness*, *Lord Jim*, and *Absalom, Absalom!* consistently pose such questions as:

> What is there to be known?; Who knows it?; How do they know it, and with what degree of certainty?; How is knowledge transmitted from one knower to another, and with what degree of reliability?; How does the object of knowledge change as it passes from knower to knower?; What are the limits of the knowable? (9)

The postmodernist novel, by contrast, embodies linguistic and narrative structures which interrogate the *ontological* status of fictional texts. To illustrate, McHale focuses on a narrative technique commonly employed by both modernists and postmodernists: framing devices, or "recursive structures," as McHale himself refers to them. According to McHale, modernist framing performs an essentially epistemological function, enabling readers to perceive truth from different, often opposing, points of reference. In postmodernist fictions, however, framing disrupts the "primary" narrative diegesis, thereby revealing the text's various ontological layers:

> Each change of narrative level in a recursive structure also involves a change of ontological level, a change of world. These embedded or nested worlds may be more or less continuous with the world of the primary diegesis, as in such Chinese-box novels as *Wuthering Heights*, *Lord Jim*, and *Absalom, Absalom!* . . . or in some cases, they may be radically different. In other words, although there is always an ontological discontinuity between the primary diegesis and hypodiegetic worlds, this discontinuity need not always be foregrounded. Indeed, in many realist and modernist novels, such as *Wuthering Heights*, *Lord Jim*, and *Absalom, Absalom!* it is rather the epistemological dimension of this structure which is foregrounded, each narrative level functioning as a link in a chain of narrative authority, reliability and unreliability, the circulation of knowledge, and so forth. So if recursive structure is to function in a postmodernist poetics of

ontology, strategies obviously must be brought to bear on it which foreground its ontological dimension. (113)

Thus, to McHale, typical postmodernist questions include:

> Which world is this?; What is a world?; What kinds of worlds are there, how are they constituted, and how do they differ?; What happens when different worlds are placed in confrontation, or when boundaries between worlds are violated?; What is the mode of existence of a text, and what is the mode of existence of the world (or worlds) it projects?; How is a projected world structured? (10)

However, if McHale's criteria are correct, how do we account for a "postmodernist" novel like Barnes' *Flaubert's Parrot*, which in endeavoring to uncover "historical" and "biographical" truths necessarily poses epistemological questions? The answer lies, in part, in the book's overt posing of these questions—in the self-conscious way, that is, in which Barnes calls attention to specific literary problems within the text itself. In Chapter 5, for example, Barnes' protagonist, Geoffrey Braithwaite, "interrupts" his narrative to explain why he dislikes "coincidences in books," arguing that "there's something cheap and sentimental about the device; it can't help seeming aesthetically gimcrack" (66). If he were a "dictator of fiction," Braithwaite exclaims, he would ban coincidences . . .

> well, perhaps not entirely. Coincidences would be permitted in the picaresque; that's where they belong. Go on, take them: let the pilot whose parachute has failed to open land in the haystack, let the virtuous pauper with the gangrenous foot discover the buried treasure—it's all right, it doesn't really matter . . .
> One way of legitimising coincidences, of course, is to call them ironies. That's what smart people do. Irony is, after all, the modern mode, a drinking companion for resonance and wit. Who could be against it? And yet sometimes I wonder if the wittiest, most resonant irony isn't just a well-polished, well-educated coincidence. (66)

In Chapter 6, Braithwaite undertakes to explain why he detests critics. He mentions having once attended a lecture delivered by Christopher Ricks, in which the distinguished Cambridge don examined the problem of whether or not factual mistakes in literature violate the artistic integrity of literary works. In one part of his lecture, Ricks pointed out that Golding's *Lord of the Flies* contains a mistake about optics. He was referring, of course, to the scene in which Piggy attempts to start a fire with his spectacles. According to Ricks, Piggy was nearsighted, which meant that the kind of eyeglasses he wore to correct that condition would have been useless in building fires. "Whichever way you held them, they would have been quite unable to make the rays of the sun converge" (77). As Braithwaite recalls, Professor Ricks, whose purpose in lecturing on this subject was to demonstrate the paradoxical interrelationship between "literariness" and factuality, concluded that if the

> factual side of literature becomes unreliable, then ploys such as irony and fantasy become much harder to use. If you don't know what's true, or what's meant to be true, then the value of what isn't true, or what isn't meant to be true, becomes diminished. (78)

Braithwaite's own conclusion, however, is that in the final analysis mistakes of this kind do not substantially affect the quality of the novel, in part because most readers are not even aware of them.

"Metafictional" digressions of this type are typical of postmodernist texts. By writing a novel which not only contains critical discussions of the kinds of literary problems that are related to the activity of fiction-making but which also features metaleptical intrusions by such historical figures as Christopher Ricks, Enid Starkie, Jean-Paul Sartre, and Gustave Flaubert, Barnes creates an ontologically multivalent text.

Another area of contention between modernists and postmodernists revolves around the problems of authority and meaning. For all their brooding over the destruction of civilization, modernists strove to articulate a controlling vision of human experience through the formal patterning of language, symbol, narrative, and mythic elements. As Alan Wilde observes in *Horizons of Assent*: "At the heart of the [modernist] enterprise one discerns the intense need to shape a disordered world—not, in the first instance, either to reform or escape it but, instead, to establish, if only negatively, a relationship with it" (47). According to Wilde, "Yeats was righter than he knew. The center has indeed not held—and for a good reason. To all intents and purposes, it has disappeared, taking with it the fulcrum on which the modernist dilemma turned or, rather, supported itself" (48). Likewise, in his discussion of modernism, Irving Howe uses such terms as "salvation of art," "quasi-religious orders of the aesthetic," "search for meaning," and "art as salvation" to characterize the modernist literary experience (153-164). The modern novelist's sense of being alienated from a bourgeois world fostered his belief in the uniqueness of his sensibility, his insights into the human condition, and his mission as an artist. Thus, in modernist literature, artistic consciousness assumes a pre-eminent position as the "shaper" or "orderer" of experiential chaos. To Robert Alter, for example, Joyce's "immense avidness for [the] reality of the nineteenth century novel" is counterbalanced by the modern recognition not only that reality is always mediated by consciousness but that consciousness itself is an artificer in constantly making something out of the formless flux of experience, inventing images and chains of connections to give it shape and substance. . . . Where things fall apart, ontologically and historically, where everything is 'worn away, age after age,' there are moments when artifice will seem not a reflection on or transformation of reality but the only reality one can count on, that one can humanly grasp. (*Partial Magic* 144)

For postmodernists, the problem with this view of the mind as creator of aesthetic order is its assumption that consciousness exists prior to language. According to Patricia Waugh:

For Sterne, as for contemporary writers, the mind is not a perfect aestheticizing instrument. It is not free, and it is as much constructed out of, as constructed with, language. The substitution of a purely metaphysical system (as in the case of Proust) or mythical analogy (as with Joyce and Eliot) cannot be accepted by the metafictionists as final structures of authority and meaning. Contemporary reflexivity implies an awareness of both language *and* metalanguage, of consciousness *and* writing. . . .

Whereas loss of order for the modernist led to the belief in its recovery at a deeper level of the mind, for metafictional writers the most fundamental assumption is that composing a novel is basically no different from composing or constructing one's reality. Writing itself rather than consciousness becomes the main object of attention. (*Metafiction* 24)

In postmodernist novels, consequently, the endeavor to achieve a cohesive vision of human reality is abandoned in favor of an articulation of "truths" which are more provisional and localized in nature.

Modernists like Eliot and Joyce have usually been seen as profoundly humanistic in their paradoxical desire for stable aesthetic and moral values, even in the face of their realization of the inevitable absence of such universals. Postmodernism differs from this, not in its humanistic contradictions, but in the provisionality of its response to them: it refuses to posit any structure or, what Lyotard calls, master narrative—such as art or myth—which, for such modernists, would have been consolatory. It argues that such systems are attractive, perhaps even necessary; but this does not make them any less illusory. (Alexander 16)

Thus, "not truth, but whose truth," becomes the central credo of postmodernist fiction, and nowhere is this relativism more pronounced than in such novels as *Flaubert's Parrot*, *A History of the World in 10 1/2 Chapters*, *Talking It Over*, and *The Porcupine*.

The purpose of this study is to examine postmodernist elements in Barnes' fiction, particularly its explorations into the relation of fiction to history and biography. While not new with Barnes, the idea that history, or more precisely, historiography, is "fictional" in nature is a persistent theme in his work, especially in *Flaubert's Parrot* and *A History of the World in 10 1/2 Chapters*. Against the traditional concept of historiography as a process of empirical documentation, and of the historiographer as one who effaces his or her subjectivity in the pursuit of objectivity and realism, postmodernism posits history as "story," the telling of which "requires the perspective of the teller, and thus the manipulative selection of detail" (Marshall 153). As Barnes points out in *A History of the World in 10 1/2 Chapters*:

> History isn't what happened. History is just what historians tell us. There was a pattern, a plan, a movement, expansion, the march of democracy; it is a tapestry, a flow of events, a complex narrative, connected, explicable. One good story leads to another. (240)

This view of history as fictive construct recalls Hayden White's own theoretical formulations on the nature of historiography. As White observes, because historical writing, like fiction, is a process of narrativization, it necessarily embodies all the traditional figures of literary expression, including metaphor, metonymy, synecdoche, and irony. According to White:

> The peculiar dialectic of historical discourse—and of other forms of discursive prose as well, perhaps even the novel—comes from the effort of the author to mediate between alternative modes of emplotment and explanation, which means, finally, mediating between alternative modes of language use or tropological strategies for originally describing a given field of phenomena and constituting it as a possible field of representation. (*Tropics of Discourse* 129)

As White suggests, far from being a mere literary embellishment, the historian's use of figurative strategies is an essential tool without which he or she could not organize the disembodied facts of the past into meaningful patterns of discourse. To White, most nineteenth-century historians

> did not realize that the facts do not speak for themselves, but that the historian speaks for them, speaks on their behalf, and fashions the fragments of the past into a whole whose integrity is—in its representation—a purely discursive one. Novelists might be dealing with imaginary events whereas historians are dealing with real ones, but the process of fusing events, whether imaginary or real, into a comprehensible totality capable of serving as the object of representation is a poetic process. Here the historian must utilize precisely the same tropological strategies, the same modalities of representing relationships in words, that the poet or novelist uses. In the unprocessed historical record and in the chronicle of events which the historian extracts from the record, the facts exist only as a congeries of contiguously related fragments. These fragments have to be put

> together to make a whole of a particular, not a general, kind. And they are put together in the same ways that novelists use to put together figments of their imaginations to display an ordered world, a cosmos, where only disorder or chaos might appear. (*Tropics* 125)

While Barnes and his postmodernist contemporaries would certainly embrace White's belief in the inherent fictiveness of historical writing, they might at the same time be disinclined to endorse his notion of history as a "comprehensible totality"—as is attested not only by Braithwaite's failure, in *Flaubert's Parrot*, to achieve a "total" documentation of Flaubert's life but also by the opposing "fabulations" which find expression in many of the stories of *A History of the World in 10 1/2 Chapters*.

Like such contemporaries as John Fowles, Salman Rushdie, and John Banville, Barnes conducts his revision of traditional modes of historical knowledge through a novelistic technique known as historiographic metafiction, a form which combines fictional reflexivity and historical narrative in order to expose the intrinsic discursiveness (and thus the concomitant ethical and epistemological limitations) of both genres. According to Brenda Marshall, postmodernism "views history as discourse, as something that is manipulated first by the teller, and then by the receiver" (152). Unlike traditional historical fiction, which assumes a direct correspondence between words and events, historiographic metafiction is characterized by a "refusal to see the past as constituted by events which we can innocently recapture or re-present through language. We no longer are able to think about absolute and unquestionable 'facts' or truths of history, speaking now of 'histories' instead of history" (147). In place of the idea of history as unitary and teleological, postmodernism affirms its multiplicity and indeterminacy. To quote Brenda Marshall again, "Historiographic metafiction recognizes the impossibility of imposing a single determinate meaning on history, on texts, on history-as-text" (174).

Thus, historiographic metafiction challenges conventional history's claim to objective authority. It had always been assumed that the historian's ability to transcribe past events into documents implied his or her intellectual "control" over those events. However, as a result of poststructuralism's revelations about the nature of language, textuality, and intertextuality, as well as its acknowledgement of our world's social, ethnic, religious, and sexual plurality, the historian has been "decentered," or deprived of his privileged position as "center" of historical knowledge:

> The poststructuralist decentering of the subject from the position from which reason emanates means that we no longer perceive of history as a linear construct which places the subject, in the present, in the privileged position of mak-

ing sense of all that has come before—as if the subject were either outside of history, or else the final moment toward which all history has marched. (Marshall 148)

What is more, as both Linda Hutcheon and Hayden White have argued, insofar as the "past" can only be known through previous documents, the historian is always at the mercy of language and textuality, and is not, as had been formerly assumed, the originator of historical meaning.

The apparent "objectivity" of traditional historical texts conveyed the impression of ideological neutrality. However, poststructuralist theory reveals that historical writing always reflects the moral, social, and political prejudices of the historian and the prevailing ideology of his or her culture. As White observes:

> The issue of ideology points to the fact that there is no value-neutral mode of emplotment, explanation, or even description of any field of events, whether imaginary or real, and suggests that the very use of language itself implies or entails a specific posture before the world which is ethical, ideological, or more generally political: not only all interpretation, but also all language is politically contaminated. (*Tropics* 129)

Consequently, postmodernist texts like *Midgnight's Children*, *Flaubert's Parrot*, and *A History of the World in 10 1/2 Chapters*—each of which implicitly poses such questions as "Whose history gets told?"; "Who tells it?"; "For what purpose?"; "Who is excluded from history?"; "Does history distort the facts?"; and "How do we know history?"—often presents alternative or dissenting versions of the past, such as those which might be told from black, gay, Jewish, Native American, colonial, or feminine perspectives.

The aim of this introduction has been to establish reasons for including Barnes in a discussion of postmodernist literature. Barnes' postmodernism is reflected in its interest in the problems of "naming" and "representation" (*Flaubert's Parrot* and *A History of the World in 10 1/2 Chapters*), its awareness of fictionality (*FP, A History*, and *Talking It Over*), its concern with the deceptions of traditional historical discourse (*FP* and *A History*), and its distrust of what Francois Lyotard has referred to as metanarratives, discourses which, either overtly or insidiously, seek to inculcate a culture's dominant moral, political, and aesthetic ideologies (*A History* and *The Porcupine*). Indeed, *Flaubert's Parrot* and *A History of the World in 10 1/2 Chapters*—Barnes' two most daring forays into "postmodernist" technique—remind us that fictionality is an "increasingly appropriate focus of attention in a culture where clear standards of truth and significance" elude formulation (Wynne-Davies, 126).

Chapter 1

Youth and Marriage

When Christopher Lloyd, the narrator and main character of Barnes' first novel, *Metroland*, finally reaches "adulthood," he finds himself enjoying the very same "bourgeois" things that he had formerly sneered at as an adolescent: marriage, home, parenthood, career, mowing lawns, and playing golf. Emboldened by what he considered to be his spiritual affinities with John Osborne and the "Angries," Christopher had channeled much of the emotional and intellectual energy of his adolescence into demonstrating his "alienation" from the older generation. One of his favorite ways of doing this was to exasperate commuters (consisting mainly of London businessmen whom Christopher referred to as "pinstripes") by beating them to their favorite seats on the morning train into the city (at this time Christopher was going to school in London). To Chris, depriving the "old fuggers" of their customary places on the shuttle was the "day's first subversive action" (59). During one of his more memorable commutes home, Christopher meets an elderly man on the train:

> He was an old sod, I thought; dead bourgeois. The embroidered sun shining out of his slippers was the nearest he got to energy and life, I thought. But he was *syphilise*. Pity he wasn't Belgian. He might be Belgian. (35)

As they ride together, the old man talks incessantly about the glory days of London's commuter rail service. Christopher is convinced that the elderly gent is a child molester:

> Used to be a great line. Used to have . . . ambitions. Heard of the Brill Line? What was he after? Rape, abduction? Better humour him, otherwise six months and I'd be plump and ball-less in Turkey. (35)

Ironically, as an adult, Christopher announces his plans to write a book about the history of London's railway systems; moreover, near the end of the novel, in a chapter in which Christopher attends a high school reunion, he describes one of his former teachers—a man who had once inspired terror in his pupils—as the sort of person for whom one would gladly relinquish one's seat on a train.

Metroland is a book of subtly and steadily accreting ironies. For instance, while growing up, Christopher had always despised Sundays—especially Sunday mornings, when the seemingly endless peeling of church bells and the heavy clanking of railroad cars from nearby Eastwick terminal would rip-saw through his drowsy early-morning reveries. By afternoon a third sound had joined in the general din: the roar of the neighbors' lawn mowers. Sundays also meant washing the family car and making that unpleasant weekly hike across the local golf course. Worst of all, Sundays seemed to drive home the fact that, at sixteen, independence from family was still only a pipe dream. By the time Christopher reaches thirty, however, these very same Sunday morning sounds and activities create a comforting sense of well-being for him. After slipping out of the house early on Sunday mornings, Christopher picks his

> way across the golf course, watching an early drive catch the dew on its first bounce and pull up quickly, glistening. I like it here; I like the misty different perspective. From high up by the fourth tee, you can follow tiny figures pulling trolleys along the fairway, and bursting into striped colour at the touch of rain. Below, smart silver trains process, with the clack of muted knitting machines; their windows flash the sun at you, like boys with playground mirrors. Churches remind other people to get up and pray. (135)

And in what appears to be a final capitulation to the pressures of suburbia (although he would have us know that he can still quote Mallarme), we learn that Christopher mows his lawn every Saturday afternoon. To Toni Barbarowski, Christopher's erstwhile school- and soulmate, his old friend's new-found domesticity effectively brings to an end the two boys' collaborative revolt against bourgeois mediocrity. Nor is the strangeness of this turn of events lost upon Christopher, for as he discovers later on, "part of growing up [is] being able to ride irony without being thrown" (135).

Metroland follows in the great tradition of the *bildungsroman*—that genre which figures so prominently in the evolution of 19th and 20th century Anglo-American fiction. However, instead of employing a continuous chronological narrative, like that found in many conventional *bildungsromane,* Barnes recounts his protagonist's coming-of-age in three parts, each of which focuses on a specific period in Christopher's life: 1963, when he is sixteen years old and living with his parents in Metroland, a suburb of London; 1968, when he is a twenty-one year old graduate student in Paris; and 1977, when he is a thirty year old husband and father. Part I centers on the adventures of Christopher and his friend Toni Barbarowski during that time of life when "everything seemed more open to analogy, to metaphor, than it does now"; "when the world yielded more meanings, more interpretations, a greater variety of available truths" (13); and when "idealism" and "carnality" co-existed in perfect balance.

As teenagers the two boys enjoy spending their free time observing people and flouting middle class mores. That these activities are carried out more in a spirit of playful mockery than earnest defiance never seems to diminish the exuberance with which the boys perform them. One senses that the boys' "scorn" is always tempered by their awareness that they are playing a role. As Christopher observes, "Our coruscating idealism expressed itself in a public pose of raucous cynicism" (15). Together the youths engage in such pastimes as "*ecraser l'infame*" (crushing the infamous—the "infamous" in this case presumably referring to members of the "establishment"); "*epater la bourgeoisie*" (dumbfounding/outraging the middle class; and the "constructive loaf" ("insouciant" observation of life). Savoring their roles as "*flaneurs*," the two teens scour the streets, shops, and railway stations of London and Metroland, preying on vendors, shoppers, churchgoers, and even prostitutes. Besides churches, which supply the youths with "vivid deceptions of faith," their favorite haunt is the National Gallery—London's center of "pure aesthetic pleasure" (29). Here the boys study the spectators' reactions to great paintings. The *modus operandi* of this particular activity is for one of the boys to study the subject with binoculars while the other records his partner's observations in a notebook. Here, for instance, is the narrator's description of a woman viewing "Van Dyck's Equestrian Portrait of Charles I":

> The gallery was fairly empty that afternoon, and the woman was quite at ease with the portrait. I had time to impart a few speculative biographical details.
> 'Dorking? Bagshot? Forty-five, fifty. Shoppers' return. Married, two children, doesn't let him fug her anymore. Surface happiness, deep discontent.'
> That seemed to cover it. She was gazing up at the picture now like an idol-worshipper. Her eyes hosed it swiftly up and down, then settled, and began to move slowly up its surface. At times, her head would cock sideways and her neck thrust forward; her nostrils appeared to widen, as if she scented new correspondences in the painting; her hands moved on her thighs in little flutters. Gradually, her movements quietened down.
> 'Sort of religious peace,' I muttered to Toni. 'Well, quasi-religious, anyway; put that.' I focussed on her hands again; they were now clasped together like an altar-boy's. Then I tilted the binoculars back up to her face. She had her eyes closed. I mentioned this.

>'Seems to be recreating the beauty of what's in front of her, or savouring the after-image; can't tell.'
>
>I kept the glasses on her for a full two minutes, while Toni, his biro raised, waited for my next comment. There were two ways of reading it: either she was beyond the point of observable pleasure; or else she was asleep. (12)

The two boys affect a kind of Oscar-Wildish bohemian disdain for philistines and other things bourgeois. They talk passionately about art and French writers, especially Baudelaire, Rimbaud, and Camus. For the boys, art is

> the constant to which one could be unfailingly devoted and which would never cease to reward; more crucially, it was the stuff whose effect on those exposed to it was ameliorative. It made people not just fitter for friendship and more civilised . . . but better—kinder, wiser, nicer, more peaceful, more active, more sensitive. If it didn't, what good was it? (29)

The two boys dedicate their lives to preserving the integrity of colors, which, according to Christopher, are

> ultimates, purities of extra value to the godless. We didn't want bureaucrats fugging around with them.
> They'd already got at
> '. . . the language . . .'
> '. . . the ethics . . .'
> '. . . the sense of priorities . . .'
> but these you could, in the last analysis, ignore. You could go your own swaggering way. But if they got at the colours? We couldn't even count on being ourselves anymore. (14–15)

Nor will the boys allow anything as vulgar as the pursuit of emoluments to tarnish their aestheticism. As Christopher points out:

> we knew by the time we were grown up, the state would be paying people like us simply to exist, simply to walk about like sandwich-men advertising the good life. But stuff like the purity of language, the perfectabilty of the self, the function of art, plus a clutch of intangibles like Love, Truth, Authenticity . . . well, that was different. (15)

As the youths lunge awkwardly toward adulthood, they display all the ungainly curiosity typical of adolescents, especially where girls and sex are concerned. Furtive images of nude women bedevil their consciences. They debate the relative merits of marrying virgins and nymphomaniacs. At school they wait in feverish anticipation for the biology instructor's lesson on human reproduction. When it becomes clear that the teacher does not intend to venture beyond the reproductive systems of rabbits, the students grumble in disappointment. At home the teens pose awkward questions about sexuality. On one such occasion, Christopher asks his mother to define "eunuch." After several torturous moments in which the woman desperately attempts to enlist the aid of her husband, she replies that a eunuch is "An Abyssinian servant." Failing to have their questions answered satisfactorily, the boys feel betrayed by their parents and the older generation.

Another "crisis" in Christopher's coming-of-age occurs when his older brother, Nigel, brings home a girlfriend. Her arrival stirs up all kinds of conflicting emotions in the younger boy. The presence of a "real" girl with his brother merely underscores his own sense of fumbling, inept childishness. As the evening unfolds, he feels resentment because Nigel and his girl pay him only the scantest attention; jealousy because his brother is old enough to have a girlfriend; and sadness because the girl is coming between his brother and him. The next day, when Christopher tells Toni about Nigel's new girlfriend, the two boys submit her to the "SST"—or "Soul," "Suffering," and "Tits"—test.

In addition to Christopher's tentative forays into the dark woods of sexual knowledge, there is his "paralyzing" fear of death, which he relates in a chapter entitled "The Big D." The onset of this fear, Christopher argues, coincided with his rejection of God—a rejection which had been prompted by the "boringness of Sundays, the creeps who took it all seriously at school, Baudelaire and Rimbaud, the pleasure of blasphemy, . . . inability any longer to think of wanking as a sin, and . . . an unwillingness to believe that dead relatives were watching what I was doing" (53). The death-fear racks him most violently at night, when in "total wakefulness" and "total aloneness within" his "pyjamaed, shaking body," Christopher ponders the meaning of non-existence and "the realisation of Time (always capitalised) going on without you for ever and ever" (54).

With the help of Toni, Christopher attempts to assuage his fear by conceiving various forms of immortality, such as immortality through one's offspring (an option which the boys dismiss when they consider how poorly they themselves have represented their own parents); immortality through art (all hope of which is dashed when the boys are introduced to the concept of "planet death": after all, they reason, "You might be able to get used to the idea of personal extinction if you thought the world went on for ever with generations of kids sitting in amazement as your works chattered through on computer printout" [55]. But with Earth's extinction in the offing, one could not even rely on art to guarantee posthumous fame); and finally, immortality as a "gruelly bit of essence nimbusing around in a Huxleyan goo" (54).

Many years later, however, Christopher discovers that his attitude toward death has changed when he attends the funeral of his Uncle Arthur. One of the book's most memorable characters, the curmudgeonly Uncle Arthur had elevated shirking to an art form. An inveterate malingerer, Arthur was famed for his skill in manipulating other people—particularly Christopher—into doing his household chores by invoking a legion of fictitious ailments. His indentured servitude notwithstanding, however, Christopher had been captivated by Uncle Arthur's resourcefulness and fiery independence. As he puts it sometime after Arthur's death, although he could not bring himself to feel love for his Uncle, he had grown to respect "the honesty of his dislike for me, and to value his warping self-sufficiency" (158). While driving home from the crematorium, Christopher reflects on his own death:

> I mused lightly about Arthur's death, about him simply not existing any more; then let my brain idle over my own future non-existence. I hadn't thought about it for years. And then I suddenly realised I was contemplating it almost without fear. I started again, more seriously this time, masochistically trying to spring that familiar trigger for panic and terror. But nothing happened; I felt calm. (161)

Each of *Metroland*'s three parts ends with a chapter entitled "Object Relations," which reveals how certain objects in Christopher's life become emblematic of his shifting expectations and states of mind. In the first of these, the adult Christopher looks back on the various objects which littered his bedroom and muses on how these objects reflected not only the physical and emotional history of his adolescence but also the dreams he had for the future. Among the numerous items he lists is a

> chair draped with the day's dumped clothes. Propped against it is a suitcase on which, every so often, I mentally stick labels. The labels indicate several generations of travel; some are grubby and tattered; all imply *l'adieu supreme des mouchoirs*. I can go; I will go. So far the case is label-less. It is all to come. One day I shall fix the real labels on myself. It is all to come. (72)

Other objects—those given to him by relatives and friends—like the bedside lamp which a "roving cousin" bought for him in Portugal, betoken the amorphous yearnings and emotions of adolescence:

> Objects redolent of all I felt and hoped for; yet objects which I myself only half-willed, only half-planned. Some I chose, some were chosen for me, some I consented to. . . . What else are you at that age but a creature part willing, part consenting, part being chosen? (72)

Part II takes place in 1968, in Paris, where Christopher is doing research for a post-graduate thesis in British influences on French theater between 1798 and 1850 (a period, Christopher later concedes, during which the British had very little influence over French theater). As Chris puts it, "I'd gone to Paris to do some research for part of a thesis I'd undertaken so that I could get a grant and go to Paris" (83). No sooner is Christopher installed in his "airy, slightly derelict studio-bedroom with a creaky French floor," than he begins to relish his new-found autonomy, and as the excitement of being a young single man in Paris begins to distract him from his academic pursuits, Christopher finds himself spending less and less time at the Bibliotheque Nationale and more and more at cafes and the Musee Gustave Moreau, an obscure little museum which "you tend to hear about . . . on your third visit [to Paris] and get around to going [to] on your fourth" (106).

While in Paris, Christopher meets a French girl named Annick, with whom he becomes so engrossed that he misses "*les evenements*," much to the consternation of his friend Toni. It is Annick's sincerity and candor as much as her beauty which attracts Christopher to her, and their brief love affair becomes a kind of turning point in his life. With their first kiss still singing on his lips, Christopher marches off to the Palais Royal feeling "impressed" with himself and remarking that

> everything was coming together, all at once. The past was all around; I was the present; art was here, and history, and now the promise of something much like love or sex. Over there in that corner was where Moliere worked; across there, Cocteau, then Colette. . . . And bringing it all together, ingesting it, making it mine, was me—fusing all the art and the history with what I might, with luck, be calling the life. (93)

After introducing her twenty-one year old virgin beau to sex, Annick begins to teach Christopher the kind of emotional and intellectual honesty that precipitates his eventual break with Toni. Christopher observes that

> When I was with her . . . it was different, easy. Her honesty was infectious. . . . Annick was the first person with whom I truly relaxed. Previously I had—even with Toni—been just honest for effect, competitively candid. Now, though the effect may have been the same to the outside observer, inside it felt different. (100)

And he adds:

> Until I met Annick I'd always been certain that the edgy cynicism and disbelief in which I dealt, plus a cowed trust in the word of any imaginative writer, were the

only tools for the painful, wrenching extraction of truths from the surrounding quartz of hypocrisy and deceit. The pursuit had always seemed something combative. Now, not exactly in a flash, but over a few weeks, I wondered if it weren't something both higher—above the supposed conflict—and simpler, attainable not through striving but a simple inward glance. (101)

Paris proves to be the young protagonist's spiritual crucible. While there he is barraged by self-doubts and conflicting emotions, many of which are triggered by his feelings for Annick, as well as by his changing relationship with Toni. Unsure if what he feels for Annick is love, Christopher nevertheless dashes off a letter to Toni informing him of his affair. Toni writes back to congratulate his former school mate on his sexual conquest and at the same time to admonish him against falling in love. The letter—a testament to Toni's consummate cynicism—ends with a promise to send Christopher a box of condoms. Though Toni's letter fails to dampen Christopher's high spirits (at least on the surface, that is; for the reader may detect a note of defensiveness in Christopher's reaction to the letter, almost as if it had induced in him the need to rationalize his feelings for Annick), it does fuel his awareness of the slowly widening rift between him and Toni. As Christopher remembers it:

> It was the sort of letter you half-read, smile at, and put aside. There's some point in advising the totally inexperienced; but advice to those on whom life has turned either sour or ridiculously sweet—it's a waste of postage. Besides, Toni and I were beginning to drift apart. The enemies who had given us common cause were no longer there; our adult enthusiasms were bound to be less congruent than our adolescent hates. (97)

All of this is complicated by Christopher's sudden emotional attachment to Marion, a young English woman whom he had met in Paris while living with Annick. With his life thus in seeming turmoil, Christopher leaves Paris. As he inventories the objects in his apartment just before departing (he does this in the "Object Relations" chapter which concludes Part II), Christopher reflects on what his experiences in Paris have meant to him. He had come to France hoping to attain an "enriching self-knowledge" and to find "the key to some synthesis between art and life" (128). But as he looks back on that last day in Paris, Christopher not only reassesses the meaning of this relationship but also puzzles over the possibility of ever achieving such a synthesis:

> Some people say that life is the thing, but I prefer reading: [Toni and I] would have endorsed that guiltily at the time, guiltily because we feared that our passion for art was the result of the emptiness of our 'lives'. How did the two concepts

interact? Where was the point of balance?. . . . Could a life be a work of art, or a work of art a higher form of life? Was art merely posh entertainment on to which a fake spiritual side had been foisted by the non-religious? (128)

As in the "Object Relations" chapter at the end of Part I, Part II's conclusion presents certain items in Christopher's Paris apartment which become associated with important events in his life—such as the bed in which he lost his virginity. And after describing other objects, Christopher takes an inventory of himself:

> The final object was me. Packed tight like my suitcase—I'd had to sit on top of me to get it all in. The moral and sensual equivalents of theatre programmes were all there, bundled up chronologically and bound with rubber bands. Look, it all happened, they said, as I riffled through them again. Look at this, and this, and this. See how you reacted here, and here. Wasn't that a bit shitty? And Christ, look at this, now if you don't feel ashamed about this, I give up on you. You do feel ashamed? That's the ticket. OK, now you can look at this one—you didn't do at all badly here; genuine sensitivity I'd say, compassion, even . . . wisdom. (130)

By the time we meet him again, in Part III, Christopher, now Marion's husband, is quite different from the young man who had delighted in scoffing at the bourgeois lifestyles of his elders. Not only has he grown apart from Toni (he is a father and "happily" married man living in his own home and working for an advertising firm, whereas Toni, now even more cynical and abrasive than he was in his adolescence, is sharing an apartment with a young woman in an "unfashionable" part of town) but he has also begun to establish ties with some of the very same ex-students whom he and Toni had taken such great pains to dissociate themselves from at school. Indeed, one of these former schoolmates offers Christopher a job as an editor in his publishing house. Another ex-classmate—whose present interests include railroad history—agrees to help Christopher with his book on London's railway systems.

But it is the apparent change in Christopher's attitude toward art which arouses Toni's deepest consternation. In the climactic conversation between Toni and Christopher near the end of the of the novel, Toni, puzzled by his friend's apparent transformation into a "bourgeois," recalls that time when the two young men still "believed that art was to do with something happening, that it wasn't all a water-colour wank" (165).

> 'Hmmn.'
>   'What do you mean, hmmn?'
>   'Don't you sometimes wonder if that's all it is?'

'Chris...' He sounded surprised, disappointed.... 'Come on, Chris, not you as well. I mean, I know I get at you a lot, but you don't really think that do you?'

For once he seemed capable of being hurt; and I for once felt disinclined to pacify him.... 'I don't know. I love all of it as much as I ever did: I read, I go to the theatre, I like pictures...'

'Dead cunts' pictures.'

'Old pictures, OK. I like it all; I always did; I just don't know whether there's any sort of direct link between it and me—whether the connection we force ourselves to believe in is really there'.... I don't deny that its all... fun, and you know, moving and all that stuff, and interesting too. But in terms of what it actually *does*, what can you say? What can you actually say in favour of the National Gallery?'

'Shit all, I agree.'

'No—agree for the right reasons. Fill it with all the stuff you like... and still what have you got? What can you say in its favour except that it keeps people off the streets; that there's a pretty low level of mugging and incest and armed robbery inside the National Gallery?'

'Aren't you being a bit literalist?' You sound like some Soviet arts commisar to me—every vork off heart must do somm gut, immediate.'

'No, because that's obviously rubbish too.'

'So what's changed? The art hasn't, boyo.... Looks like a sell-out job to me.'

'That's a pretty silly remark.'

'Well, what's become of you? I mean, even when you were in Paris...'

'Which is a decade ago. Which is all my adult life ago.'

'Uh—a new definition of "adult": the time during which one has sold-out.'

'I told you—in the garden the other week—I just don't see that it [art] makes anything happen. Very nice for us that the Renaissance occurred and all that; but it's all really ego and aggro, isn't it?'

Toni put on his pedagogue voice again.

'You don't think the effect might be cumulative?'

'I see that it could be; but that doesn't make it any less theoretical. Either way, it seems to depend on an act of faith—and for the moment I've lapsed.'

'Another triumph for the bourgoeis steam-roller,' Toni noted sadly, almost to himself.

'You're wrong.'

'Wife, baby, reliable job, mortgage, flower garden... can't fool me.'

'What evidence is that? You're not exactly Rimbaud yourself are you?' (165–167)

What Toni has apparently failed to see is that while under the tutelage of Annick and Marion, Christopher had begun to shed his adolescent "dilettantism"; thus, by the time he reaches thirty, his youthful enthusiasm for art (while still alive to some extent) has been tempered not only by a desire to achieve greater balance in his life-experience but also by his recognition of the importance of interpersonal relations, especially those between husband and wife and parent and child.

The emotional and intellectual sincerity that Christopher discovers in Annick and Marion is one aspect of a theme which finds expression in both Parts II and III: constancy/truthfulness between friends, lovers, and spouses. Christopher's desire to maintain monogamous relationships first with Annick and later with Marion becomes a measure of his maturity. With both women, however, Christopher will find himself in the awkward position of appearing to have been unfaithful when in fact he has never cheated on either woman. According to Christopher, Marion "made me feel slightly dishonest even when I was telling the truth. But then, Annick did the same. Was this a coincidence, or was it how all girls made you feel?" (118).

The first time this happens to Christopher is when he tries to tell Annick that he has befriended three English youths, one of whom is a woman named Marion (his future wife). Even though Christopher had seen quite a lot of Marion (despite his painstaking attempt both to avoid Englishmen and suppress his "Britishness" while living in Paris), he had never had sexual relations with her, and as he tries to assuage his uneasiness about this new friendship by explaining it to Annick, he comes off looking and sounding guilty. What begins as a casual discussion about a film Christopher and Annick plan on seeing later that evening soon escalates into an argument which ends their relationship:

> 'Oh, yes,' I said casually, '*mon amie anglaise* has seen [the film]. She'(cunning confirmation of gender) 'thought it was quite good.' (Marion hadn't actually seen the film. Shit—a lie to tell the truth; where did this leave you?)
> 'OK, shall we go then?'
> I thought I better make things quite clear.
> 'Yes, *mon amie anglaise* really thought it was quite good.'
> 'Fine, that's settled, then.'
> It didn't seem settled to me. We didn't seem to be getting anywhere.
> '*Mon amie anglaise* . . . '
> 'You want to tell me something?'
> ' . . . ?'
> 'Is this *le tact anglais*?' . . . I hadn't seen this—almost fierceness—on her face before. This was new. 'What? No. What do you mean?'
> 'Do you want to tell me something?'
> 'Um . . . This. . .This film is . . . apparently very good.
> 'Yes. How do you know?'
> 'Oh, one of my friends told me.'
> Genderless again; also hopeless. Instead of being casual and throwaway, it was coming out furtive and nervous.

> 'I thought you mentioned an English girl friend.'
> 'Uh, nnn, yes, I did. Why, don't you have any French boy friends?'
> 'Yes, but I don't usually refer to one of them three times running unless I want to say something particular about him.'
> 'Well, I suppose all I wanted to say about . . . about *cette amie anglaise* is that . . . she's a friend.'
> 'You mean you're sleeping with her.' Annick stubbed out her cigarette and glared at me.
> 'No, of course not. I sleep with you.'
> 'So you do. I had noticed it from time to time. But not twenty-four hours a day.'
> 'I'm not . . . perfidious.' (I couldn't think of the word for "unfaithful"; for some reason, only *adultere* came into my head, which had quite the wrong implications.) (120--121)

When Christopher compounds the problem by saying "*Je t'aime bien*" to Annick instead of "*Je t'aime,*" she bursts into tears and flies out the door, leaving Christopher alone to ponder the enigmas of love ("When do you cross the dividing line? When does *Je t'aime bien* become *Je t'aime*?"). His reflections on Annick's flight reveal the power of language: "Doesn't the terminology affect the emotion in any case? Shouldn't I just have said '*Je t'aime*' (and who's to say I wouldn't have been telling the truth)? Naming can lead to making" (125).

A second occasion on which Christopher finds himself defending his sexual "constancy"—this time to his wife—occurs the day after a young woman had tried to seduce him at a party hosted by one his ex-schoolmates. Even though Christopher was able to fend off her sexual advances, the encounter left him feeling guilty. As he tries to explain the incident to Marion, Christopher's circumspection is put to rout by his wife's rather disarming directness:

> 'I suppose I was thinking, well, if we're both about thirty now: it was all in general terms really—I suppose I was wondering if we were going to end up sleeping with other people ever?'
> 'You mean, you were wondering if you were. . . . And the answer is, of course you will . . . .'
> 'Oh come on . . .' But why did I look away? I felt guilty already, as if she was calmly showing me Polaroids of my humping bum.
> 'Of course you will. I mean, probably not now, not here; not, I hope to God, ever in this house. But some time. I've never doubted that. Sometime. It's too interesting not to.
> 'But I haven't tried to, I haven't wanted to.' I felt upset as well as guilty. . . .
> 'It's all right, Chris. You didn't go into marriage expecting a virgin and I didn't go in expecting a flagrantly faithful husband. Don't think I can't imagine what it's like to be sexually bored.' (162)

As the interview continues, Marion reveals that she herself had engaged in a brief extra-marital affair:

> 'And so, even if you aren't asking, you may as well know that the answer is Yes I did once, and Yes it was only once, and No it didn't make any difference to us at the time as we weren't getting on perfectly anyway, and No I don't particularly regret it, and No you haven't met him or heard of him.'
> Christ. Shit. Fuck. She looked at me, directly, openly, with calm eyes.
> I was the one who looked away. It was all wrong.
> 'And I've never been tempted since, and with Amy now I shouldn't think I will be, and it's all right, Chris, it's really all right.'
> Shit. Piss. Fuck. . . .
> What was I meant to feel? What did I feel? That it was quite funny really. Also, that it was interesting. Also, that I was half-proud that Marion was still capable of astonishing me. Jealousy, anger, petulance?
> They could hang around for later. (163)

I have quoted Christopher and Marion's conversation at some length because it represents—along with that of the relation of art to life—one of Barnes' most recurrent themes: marriage. Indeed, this theme figures so prominently in such works as *Metroland*, *Before She Met Me*, *Flaubert's Parrot*, and *Talking it Over* that together they form what might be described as a "marriage group" (even though *Talking It Over* was written much later than the other three novels). Because of the "apocalyptic" thematic character of much postmodernist fiction, as well as of the prodigious creative energy which contemporary novelists have invested in narrative experimentation, one might be tempted to regard Barnes' reprising of the "marriage" theme—a theme which dominates 19th century realist fiction—as obsolete, even as it finds expression in some of his more "postmodernist" works. But whereas in the classic realist novel marriage is often used to effect narrative resolution, Barnes' treatment of this theme is much more problematical in character. As David Higdon observes: "Barnes is drawn to the topics of estrangement, obsession and the power of the past; however, Barnes pursues these topics through a growing concentration on adultery" (175). For example, in *Before She Met Me*, another novel which exemplifies contemporary fiction's preoccupation with the relationship between art and life, Barnes chronicles the gradual erosion of his protagonist's sanity. Graham Hendrick, an otherwise unassuming and thoroughly "civilized" individual, becomes the victim of a consuming jealousy which impels him to commit murder and suicide. The object of this jealousy is his second wife, a former movie actress named Ann Mears. Just how Ann inspires this emotion in her husband is the main theme of the book, and the driving force behind the novel's peculiarly obsessive character.

Graham, an academic historian who in effect extrapolates his wife's sexual "history" from her film performances, is jealous of the male actors with whom Ann has made love on the screen (and in some cases off the screen as well). He fuels this jealousy with repeated viewings of Ann's love scenes at local (and some not so local) movie theaters, and, of course, the more he sees, the more obsessive he becomes. In no time at all Graham begins to bring all the tools of his trade to bear on his investigation into Ann's past—ransacking books, maps, and films—anything that will provide information about Ann's past romances. Gripped by what he describes as a "retrospective" jealousy, Graham conceives two categories of male actors—those who have slept with Ann only on screen and those who have slept with her both on and off-screen. What is more, with the help of atlases and travel brochures, Graham conjures up a whole geography of his wife's sexual liaisons. While planning a summer vacation itinerary with Ann, Graham pours over maps of various European countries, mentally eliminating all those places that Ann might have visited with her ex-lovers. After discounting the entire continent of Europe, Graham finally alights on the idea of travelling to India, a country he feels is not haunted by Ann's former boy friends:

> There was not a single Indian in India, he reflected, who had ever seen Ann walking side by side with someone who wasn't him. That was a solid, unshiftable fact. It left, of course, all the Indians in England, Italy, Los Angeles, the South of France, Spain and Germany, any number of whom might have seen her arm in arm with Benny or Chris or Lyman or Phil or whoever. But these Indians were vastly outnumbered by Indian Indians, absolutely none of whom (except perhaps on an overseas holiday—now that was a thought) could ever possibly have so seen her. (58)

The odd thing about Graham's jealousy, of course, is that it springs from his apparent inability to separate Ann's screen persona from her "real" life. It is, after all, Ann's "fictional" love-making which initially arouses Graham's animosity. The paradox implicit in having, as central character, a historian who predicates his theoretical conclusions on cinematic "fiction" rather than on empirical "fact" embodies the contemporary novel's concern with the problematical relationship between fiction and historiography. As we shall see, each of Barnes' main characters—Graham, Ann, and novelist Jack Lupton—takes his turn at "rewriting" or "fictionalizing" history: Graham, in the fiction-based jealousy which distorts his view of Ann's earlier life—the life she lived before meeting Graham; Ann, in her failure to tell Graham about her previous love affair with Jack; and Jack, in his fictional "reconstructions" of reality.

Moreover, Graham's "metaleptical" blurring of his wife's "film" and "real life" identities recalls other texts—such as Puig's *Kiss of the Spider Woman*, Rushdie's *Midnight's Children*, and Coover's *A Night at the Movies*—whose use of cinematic techniques and terminology serves to expose (and explore) the various ontological levels implicit in any act of fictional representation—a narrative method which is perhaps most vividly demonstrated in Woody Allen's *The Purple Rose Of Cairo*. When the male lead of that film's "movie-within-a-movie" steps out of the screen in order to be with the "real life" female viewer who has fallen in love with him, he is also crossing what Brian McHale has described as "ontological borders."

In Before She Met Me, illusion gradually becomes the constitutive force of Graham's reality, as the boundaries between art and life shift and eventually dissolve in his mind, allowing his wife's screen image to assume an increasingly dominant role in his emotional and perceptual experience. Soon lurid scenarios of sexual promiscuity involving his wife and her male leads take shape in his mind; his imagination, inflamed by suspicion, becomes a battlefield of film images and reality, and it is not long before Graham's waking obsessions begin to spill over into his dreams:

> The carwash dream was compered by Larry Pitter, with whom Ann committed adultery in *The Rumpus*, a street-gang movie Graham had managed to catch twice in the last week. [In the dream] Pitter sat behind his desk smoking. . . . The door opened and three men walked in. Each in his different way struck Graham as dirty and malign. . . . 'Anyway [says Pitter], I'm sure Ann did quite the right thing at the time. Told you about me, didn't tell you why we called her the Carwash girl.' The three villains behind him chuckled. 'Now stop me if I'm boring you, Graham, but you see, what she really liked wasn't just me. It was all of us. All of us at the same time. Doing different things to her. I won't be specific, I know these things can be hurtful; I'll just leave you to imagine it. But the first time she got us all to do things to her at the same time, we were all sort of swarming all over her, licking her and stuff, she said it was just like being in a carwash. So we called her the Carwash Girl. And we used to giggle about what would happen when she met Mr. Right. Only we used to call him Mr. Carwash. I mean, she made it quite plain that it was the more the merrier as far as she was concerned. And how would any husband cope with that, we wondered. Unless, of course, there's more to you than meets the eye.' Pitter grinned. (88–89)

Having enabled him to compile a fairly exhaustive list of possible film lovers, Graham's compulsive investigation into Ann's past ends in his discovery of her affair with Jack Lupton, a long-time friend of Graham and popular author of pulp fiction. Graham's initial suspicions about his wife and Jack had been aroused one evening at a party in which Graham spotted his friend making advances toward Ann. Delirious with jealousy, Graham spends the very next day skimming through Ann's collection of Lupton's novels, searching for clues to confirm his suspicions. Needless to say, he finds them. Lupton, an inveterate womanizer, had evidently seasoned his pot-boilers with enough thinly disguised—though to Graham unmistakable—references to Ann to convince Graham of his wife's liaison with Jack. Pushed over the edge by this discovery, Graham sates his irrational lust for vengeance by stabbing Jack to death and then turning the knife on himself.

One interesting aspect of *Before She Met Me* is its intertextual inscription of *Othello*. Except for the fact that Ann, the novel's "Desdemona" figure, is not killed and that Jack, the "Cassio" figure, is, the novel bears comparison with Shakespeare's play. Like Desdemona, for instance, Ann is innocent of adultery (while she is married to Graham); and like Othello, Graham's jealousy is fuelled, in part, by the machinations of his vindictive first wife, the Iago-like Barbara. It is she who not only initiates Graham's jealousy by sending him to see the film in which he first views Ann's lovemaking but also fans his anxiety by constantly alluding to Ann's "tarnished" past.

In this same connection, Mark Millington and Alison Sinclair, in a provocative essay, suggest that *Before She Met Me* descends from a long tradition of "cuckold" literature. According to Millington and Sinclair, this tradition—inaugurated by Chaucer ("The Miller's" and "Merchant's" Tales) and Boccaccio and encompassing many other works, most notably *Othello*, *Don Quixote*'s inset story "Tale of the Ill-Advised Curiosity," *Madame Bovary*, and *Anna Karenina*—explores and ultimately deconstructs the myths of male sexual dominance which underlie patriarchal cultures.

As Millington and Sinclair point out, literary works have traditionally depicted the betrayed husband in two ways—as the "cuckold" (usually an elderly man whose loss of sexual potency does not deter him from marrying a young woman), and as the "man of honour," the husband who is "admired for his attitude and action in the face of his wife's infidelity" (1). Unlike the "cuckold," whose "foolishness" in marrying a woman much younger than he incurs society's ridicule, the "man of honour" succeeds in gaining his society's approval by killing both his wife and her lover. Thus, whereas the "man of honour"'s "authority" over women is left intact by his brutal act of vengeance, the "cuckold"'s is forfeited both by his failure to satisfy his wife's sexual needs and his unwillingness or inability to put an end to her adulteries (in those few instances when he is even aware of them). According to Millington and Sinclair, both paradigms of the betrayed husband embody gender stereotypes which reflect the organizing principle of patriarchal societies: the husband's need to enter into a monogamous relationship with a woman in order to control her sexuality—a sexuality which the husband perceives as a threat to his masculinity and by extension to the orderliness of his society.

In *Before She Met Me*, Graham Hendrick both embodies and diverges from these paradigms. At times he resembles the "cuckold," especially in his feeling of inadequacy when he is making love to Ann, who, while not totally unsatisfied with Graham as a lover, has had enough prior sexual experience to intimidate him:

> The anxiety which Graham feels about his relation with Ann appears to derive firstly from his feeling of being a cuckold or anticipating that danger . . . ; and secondly . . . from fear of her sexuality. This second area has its roots in her strong, independent past: she has known other men before Graham and therefore may have points of comparison by which to judge Graham, and she has experience that will allow her to take the initiative in their sexual relations. (Millington 14–15)

In his violent reaction to what he perceives as Ann's infidelity, however, Graham fulfills the "man of honour" role.

But there are also important ways in which Graham departs from both betrayed-husband models. He departs from the "cuckold" role, for instance, simply by virtue of the fact that his wife is not cuckolding him. As Millington and Sinclair explain: "Ann's 'infidelity' is unorthodox, since it takes place prior to the moment at which she could be unfaithful to him, in other words, before she met him" (14). Furthermore, since Ann's "adulteries" took place in the past, Graham does not receive "a public humiliation. . . . He alone construes the past as 'infidelity'" (14). Moreover, to the extent that he directs his violence against Jack and himself (he does not harm Ann), Graham also departs from the "man of honour" model:

> Jack has been identified by Graham as a current rival. Through reading Jack's novels as though he were reading history . . . , Graham decides that Jack is guilty of still having an affair with Ann: again, as with his film-going, fiction is the basis of his action. In killing Jack, Graham appears to be acting as the classic man of honour. But in killing himself, rather than Ann, he is not. In taking himself as an object of violence and leaving Ann, Graham is not simply attempting to restore the integrity of his position by eliminating perceived threats to his control. . . . his suicide seems to suggest a continuing sense of inadequacy—to that extent Graham appears not to have moved out of the sphere of the cuckold. (15)

The point which Millington and Sinclair are trying to make is that patriarchal societies are founded on self-destructive codes of behavior. By trapping men in certain kinds of roles, patriarchies deny men adequate means to express their emotions:

> Graham has certain expectations of himself deriving from his position within a patriarchal society: he wishes to lay claim to traditional, exclusive 'rights' as a husband. But his problem is that he cannot succeed in the role of husband (as he conceives it) with either his first wife, Barbara, or Ann. In this sense, he has expectations (of cultural derivation) about his masculinity which he fails to fulfil. Graham emerges therefore as a product and a victim of patriarchy. Patriarchy provides certain controls, delimits the areas of gender activity, and confers power on men, but in doing so it inevitably breaks down, if the areas are (or are perceived to be) infringed, or if men fail to achieve the power made available to them, then all that patriarchy seems to leave open to men are violent reactions and retribution, whether against others or the self: the attempt to enforce conformity. Graham shows that patriarchy cannot deal well with hurt in men. . . . (16)

That Barnes' treatment of marriage departs dramatically from its treatment in 19th century realist texts is, I think, abundantly clear from the preceding exposition. Even in a novel like *Metroland*, where the marriage-bond seems firmly intact, Christopher and Toni find themselves brooding over the "thought of Shakespeare, Moliere, and other authorities," all of whom "agreed that the ridiculous husband was not something to be laughed at" (25). And after Christopher is married, Toni persists in exposing the chinks in his friend's matrimonial armor by suggesting that his sexual constancy is grounded not in honor, but in fear.

Another interesting feature of the books which comprise Barnes' "marriage group" is the subtle way in which Barnes weaves the marriage theme into his exploration of the relationship between art and life. In *Metroland*, for instance, Christopher's increasing sense of domestic security co-extends with his changing attitudes toward art. In *Before She Met Me*, Graham's "retro-active" jealousy derives not from actually catching his wife making love with another man, or from hearing about such a thing from a third-party, but from watching her perform sexual acts in her movies. In *Talking It Over*, two men—one a "practical" businessman, the other an artsy, but impecunious, "wordsmith,"—marry the same woman successively. And in *Flaubert's Parrot*, Geoffrey Braithwaite, a man who searches for reality in fiction—only to find fiction in reality—hopes to deflect the anguish he feels over his wife's sexual indiscretions and subsequent suicide by constructing a "biography" of Flaubert—the "master of creative adultery," as critic Alison Lee describes him.

Chapter 2

Flaubert's Parrot

In his illuminating study of the self-conscious novel, *Partial Magic*, Robert Alter argues that the increasingly reflexive nature of postmodernist fiction embodies contemporary man's quest for greater self-awareness and his need to discover the underlying elements of both his personal and communal values. According to Alter, recent fiction's experimentation with language and narrative form, its obsession with literary artifice, and its penchant for self-display, make possible a climate of critical incredulity which induces the reader to examine the very intellectual, aesthetic, and ideological foundations of his or her culture. As Alter observes:

> Our culture, a kind of Faust at the mirror of Narcissus, is more and more driven to uncover the roots of what it lives with most basically—language and its origins, human sexuality, the workings of the psyche, the inherited structures of the mind, the underlying patterns of social organization, the sources of value and belief, and, of course, the nature of art. (220)

Certainly, it is this same spirit which informs Barnes' entire literary enterprise. For instance, with *Flaubert's Parrot*, a book which thematizes the relation of fiction to historiography, Barnes takes his place in the ongoing debate between poststructuralist linguistics and traditional "realist" theories of language. Like much contemporary literature, Barnes' work

> reflects the structuralist and poststructuralist scepticism about the ability of language to refer to a non-linguistic reality, and the sense that fictionality is an attribute of forms of discourse other than fiction, such as history and the social sciences. (Wynne-Davies 126)

Through his use of narrative methods which, according to Linda Hutcheon, simultaneously establish and subvert conventional structures of mimetic representation (*A Poetics* 20), Barnes is able to challenge traditional realist presuppositions about the nature of language, particularly with regard to its ability to reflect "reality." Insofar as words, being artificial symbolic constructs, can never directly reflect the intrinsic nature of the objects they purport to name, it follows that there can be no one-to-one correspondence between language and the empirical world. Consequently, since, as many poststructuralist theorists have maintained, we "create" or "invent" our world linguistically, it can be argued with some plausibility that "reality" itself is a fictional construct. In her exposition of Derrida's linguistic theories, Brenda Marshall notes that Derrida speaks of the

> moment in which a belief in representation is no longer consistent with a recognition that words do not naturally re-present things (that is, the original thing is not re-presented by its stand-in, the word); rather, words refer to other words. The result is an inflation of language. Reality is defined by the words chosen to describe it. This is what we mean when we say that reality exists as a function of the discourse that articulates it: we perceive what we know as reality through a particular system of references which in effect preconstitute the meaning of the world, and thus, the world itself. (68)

As the narrator of *Flaubert's Parrot* explains: "We no longer believe that language and reality 'match up' so congruently—indeed, we probably think that words give birth to things as much as things give birth to words." For Alison Lee, this acknowledgement of the problematic nature of language serves to undermine the legitimacy of conventional historiography and historical fiction:

> The idea of history as discursive practice is informed by the linguistic theories which challenge the traditional position that language is transparent, that the word is the direct means to the thing it represents, and that the connection between them is natural and ideologically neutral.
>
> Postmodern novels use history as both a reference to the 'real' world, and as a text or discursive construct. This differs substantially from the use of history in the traditional historical novel, where history, as a group of facts which exists extra-textually and which can be represented as it really was, is never questioned. (35)

Since its publication in 1984, *Flaubert's Parrot* has proven to be as resistant to precise generic classification as that other great riddle to literary pigeon-holers, Sterne's *Tristram Shandy*—and arguably for some of the very same reasons. "Is it a novel?" queries one French commentator. "Yes, if you want it to be. But Julian Barnes has invented a new literary genre. His parrot is by turns a narrative, a chronicle, a critical work, and an intimate journal. It is a boiling pot in which the author has mixed genres" (Salgas 15).

Blending fiction, biography, and literary criticism, *Flaubert's Parrot* explores the perimeters of fiction and reality and demonstrates—chiefly through its own narrative dislocations, multiple viewpoints, and overlapping genres—how art and life interact. In this, his third novel, Barnes abandons the chronological plot structure of conventional realist fiction for one which digresses, teases, breaks off, interrupts itself, and makes use of alternating narrative voices and shifting planes of reference, in a manner somewhat reminiscent of Sterne's *Tristram Shandy*. In Richard Todd's words, *Flaubert's Parrot* is "palimpsestically constructed, and although chapterized bears no 'narrative' in the conventional sense" (121). Indeed, in one chapter Braithwaite relinquishes control of the narrative altogether and allows Louise Colet—Flaubert's long-time mistress—to describe her turbulent relationship with Flaubert in her own words. In other sections of the book, Barnes alternates first- and third-person points-of-view in order to dispel the illusion of narrative continuity which conventional linear plot structuring makes possible. An early example of this technique can be observed in the first two chapters, in which the first-person narrative line established in chapter one—a sort of exposition chapter introducing us to the narrator and the initial conflict—is suddenly aborted in chapter two, which presents biographical "chronologies" narrated in the third-person. These strategies, combined with the book's overt intertextual inscription of *Madame Bovary*, allow Barnes to undermine such traditional novelistic techniques as temporal linearity and narrative closure.

Flaubert's Parrot also reveals the influence of Poststructuralism's rejection of traditional literary "authority." This is the notion, commonly assumed to be a pervasive factor in both the creation and reception of 19th century realist fiction, that writers and readers shared the same basic moral values, cultural traditions, and world view. As Marguerite Alexander explains:

> The great English and American novelists of the nineteenth century shared with their readers certain assumptions—about the ultimate value of society, whatever specific criticisms of it might be made; about the place of the individual within that society; about the existence, if not of God, then of a body of universal truths which included an agreed concept of human nature. (4)

Because of this tacit agreement between the writer and reader of 19th century novels, omniscient narration assumed greater importance not only as a technical device which welded the text's various narrative strands into a coherent whole but also as a vehicle for moral instruction. The 19th century reader's sense of propriety was flattered by an imperious authorial voice which resolved crises by meting out punishments to the wicked and rewards to the innocent. Moreover, the cohesive linear plot structure of 19th century fiction was thought to reflect a similarly cohesive world or moral order, its unbroken narrative surface representing a similar quality in man's social reality.

However, with the 20th century's emerging awareness of cultural plurality (gender conflicts, sexual orientation, ethnicity, and ethical relativism) it became apparent to writers that the kind of thematic and narrative cohesion which it was once presumed authorial omniscience lent to fiction was no longer valid. The "broken" narrative surfaces we witness in much contemporary fiction seem to reflect the writer's belief that an "author" is no longer in a position to impose his or her own moral vision on the world and that the contemporary novel can no longer be regarded as a representation of reality, but as a kind of reality, albeit a fictional one, in its own right. According to Marguerite Alexander:

> Moral instruction and entertainment were the two imperatives of the classical realist novel, both abandoned by the modernists in favour of an aesthetic foregrounding which had an oblique bearing on moral issues only in as far as the reader's perceptions of external reality were altered by the aesthetic experience. A good deal of postmodernist writing marks a return to moral enquiry—almost certainly in response to recent history—but in a world where moral issues are perceived to be more complex and the writer is more reticent about authorizing a particular moral position. (14)

The problematizing of novelistic "authority" derives, in part, from poststructuralism's attack on the liberal humanist concept of the "subject" as a stable, unified, and self-determining psychological entity. For poststructuralists, the individual's "self" is fluid and multiple, comprising many different "subject positions": gender, social class, race, etc. The discursive (ideological) nature of these positions renders the self unstable, contingent, and subject to the same transformations as any linguistic formation. As Alison Lee explains, "subjectivity is not a fixed, pre-linguistic essence, but an open process which is perpetually in the process of construction, thrown into crisis by alternation in language and the social formation" (55). Lee goes on to argue that

> the issues of individuality and identity are vital for historiographic metafiction, which simultaneously creates and subverts the Realist convention of an unproblematically constituted, individual 'subject' who is the prime mover of events, and from whom essential meaning emanates. (55)

This is clearly evident in *Flaubert's Parrot*, where the narrator, far from being an "autonomous source of meaning" (Lee 55), puzzles not only over the riddles of the past but also over the riddles of his own identity. Throughout the novel, the narrator's persistent failure to impose any kind meaning on either his own "history" or Flaubert's undermines humanism's faith in the constructive powers of the human self. Indeed, for David Higdon, Barnes' protagonist expresses his bewilderment in a way which makes him quite different from other protagonists. According to Higdon, *Flaubert's Parrot* features "a new type of narrator, the *reluctant narrator*, who is reliable in strict terms, indeed often quite learned and perceptive, but who has seen, experienced or caused something so traumatic that he must approach the telling of it through indirections, masks and substitutions" (174). The "indirections" and "substitutions" which Barnes' narrator uses to recount his trauma—the "trauma" being his wife's marital infidelity and subsequent "suicide" (it is strongly hinted that as his wife's physician the narrator ordered her off life-sustaining equipment after she took an over-dose of pills)—are the life of Flaubert. As Higdon observes, Barnes' protagonist displaces his personal history "onto Flaubert and creates a literary investigation to escape his own fears of having been already inscribed or scripted by Flaubert" (180).

Perhaps one of the most striking things about Barnes' "novel," apart from its rather daring appropriation of biographical material, is its singularly unpromising plot—a plot which at first belies the book's deeper narrative, thematic, and psychological complexities, as the following brief summary will, I hope, make clear.

During a trip to France's Normandy Coast—taken, ostensibly, to enable him to relive his part in the D-Day invasion of Europe—Barnes' narrator, a widower and retired British physician named Geoffrey Braithwaite, visits Rouen (in an interview with the French journal *La Quinzaine Litteraire*, Barnes claimed that his original plan was to make his narrator a novelist, but that he changed his mind about this apparently because he felt uncomfortable with the "Gidean" infinite mirror trick, whereby a novelist [Barnes himself], using a novelist as a narrator, writes a novel about another novelist. [Salgas 17]). While in Rouen, Braithwaite, a "lay" Flaubert enthusiast, tours the French novelist's birthplace, The Hotel-Dieu. Formerly a hospital, now a converted museum, The Hotel-Dieu contains, in addition to various memorabilia guaranteed to delight any devotee of Flaubert, an exhibition of sundry 18th and 19th century medical apparatus. This juxtaposition of the literary and the medical, while at first striking the narrator as somewhat incongruous, takes on a kind of ironical significance once he recalls

> Lemot's famous cartoon of Flaubert dissecting Emma Bovary. It shows the novelist flourishing on the end of a large fork the dripping heart he has triumphantly torn from his heroine's body. He brandishes the organ aloft like a prize surgical exhibit, while on the left of the drawing the feet of the recumbent, violated Emma are just visible. The writer as butcher, the writer as sensitive brute. (7)

Savoring this irony—an irony underscored, perhaps, not only by the fact that Flaubert's father and brother were both prominent Rouen physicians but also by the fact that Flaubert himself is said to have wielded the pen the way a surgeon wields a scalpel—Braithwaite continues his tour of the museum. In one of the rooms he spots a stuffed parrot, the very same parrot, his guide informs him, which had served as the original inspiration for Loulou, Felicite's beloved bird in Flaubert's story "A Simple Heart."

Some days later, while touring Flaubert's house in the neighboring village of Croisset (actually all that remains of this building by the time Braithwaite visits is a small pavilion, the rest of the house having been torn down to make room for a paper factory—an irony which, once again, is not lost upon the narrator), Braithwaite discovers another stuffed parrot. Puzzled by the appearance of this second bird, he questions the curator about the parrot he had seen at the Hotel-Dieu, whereupon the Croisset guide, bristling with jealousy and defensiveness, replies that her parrot is the authentic one. In a state of bewilderment, Braithwaite leaves Croisset determined to resolve the discrepancy.

And so begins the narrator's quest for truth—a quest which will find him criss-crossing the French countryside, writing letters, reading documents, and interviewing Flaubert authorities. Presumably, by identifying the real parrot, Braithwaite believes that he will be able to gain greater insight into Flaubert's life and art. According to one critic, Braithwaite is convinced that "an apprehension of the parrot will decipher an entire set of codes, unlocking the secrets of the Flaubert system" (White 113). His journey ends almost exactly where it began—back in Rouen; this time, however, in the upper chamber of the city's museum, where Flaubert had originally procured the stuffed parrot, and where Braithwaite is now permitted to examine three other stuffed parrots—each of which might be considered as the model for Loulou's inspiration; and after his painstaking attempt to authenticate one of the two original birds he had seen, this is precisely the conclusion Braithwaite arrives at: perhaps one of the stuffed parrots locked away in this top floor is the authentic one. That we can never know for sure is precisely Barnes' point, and the dilemma Braithwaite finds himself in at the end of his "narrative" is in actuality the answer to the question which the novel implicitly poses: if the little details in an individual's life elude our ability to understand them, then how can we expect to grasp the larger, more significant ones? As Braithwaite puts it:

> How do we seize the past? How do we seize the foreign past? We read, we learn, we ask, we remember, we are humble; and then a casual detail shifts everything. Flaubert was a giant; they all said so. He towered over everybody like a strapping Gallic chieftan. And yet he was only six feet tall: . . . . Tall, but not gigantic; shorter than I am, in fact, and when I am in France I never find myself towering over people like a French chieftan. . . . [So] the giants were not so tall (were the dwarfs therefore shorter too?). . . . How can we know such trivial, crucial details? We can study files for decades, but every so often we are tempted to throw up our hands and declare that history is merely another literary genre: the past is autobiographical fiction pretending to be a parliamentary report. (94)

As the novel unfolds and Braithwaite continues his investigation, Barnes' eponymous parrot begins to take on a multiplicity of meanings, referring by turns to Felicite's beloved bird, a kind of architectural structure, a restaurant named after a parrot, language (parrots being the birds which imitate human speech without knowing the meaning of what they imitate), and finally the pursuit of truth itself (for just as there are many parrots by the end of the novel, so are there many ways of apprehending the truth or, better still, many truths to be apprehended). For Alison Lee, the "parrot's" semantic versatility reflects the fact that "language is inescapably plural" (39).

As we saw earlier, *Flaubert's Parrot*, like many contemporary novels, contains a variety of "self-destruct" mechanisms—narrative strategies which Barnes uses to undermine the conventional structures of fictional verisimilitude. One of these mechanisms—metafiction—is a literary technique which calls attention to the act of writing itself in order to show that fictions are just that—fictions—and not exact representations of reality or embodiments of ultimate truths. Indeed, as Alsion Lee observes in her book *Realism and Power: Postmodern British Fiction*, metafiction "questions the Realist assumption that truth and reality are absolutes" (3). In *Metafiction: The Theory and Practice of Self-Conscious Fiction* critic Patricia Waugh argues that

> Metafiction explicitly lays bare the conventions of realism; it does not ignore or abandon them. Very often, realistic conventions supply the 'control' in metafictional texts, the norm or background against which the experimental strategies can foreground themselves. More obviously, of course, this allows for a stable level of readerly familiarity, without which the ensuing dislocations might be either totally meaningless or so outside the normal modes of literary or non-literary

communication that they cannot be committed to memory. . . . Metafiction, then, does not abandon the 'real world' for the narcissistic pleasures of the imagination. What it does is to reexamine the conventions of realism in order to discover—through its self-reflection—a fictional form relevant and comprehensible to contemporary readers. In showing us how literary fiction creates its imaginary worlds, metafiction helps us understand how the reality we live day by day is similarly constructed, similarly 'written.' (45)

While not as radically metafictional as the works of such writers as Robert Coover, John Barth, and Donald Barthelme—Barnes' novels occasionally display what Patricia Waugh might describe as the metafictionists' strategy of setting in opposition those linguistic and narrative elements which "construct" illusions of reality, in the manner of classic 19th century realist fiction, and those which "deconstruct" them à la Borges, Nabokov, and Robbe-Grillet, etc. Unlike the 19th century realist writer, whose narrative techniques presupposed a direct relationship between language and reality (a presupposition which in turn ensured both the inviolability of the novelist's moral vision and the integrity of the rhetorical and narrative structures with which he articulated that vision), most "postmodernist" authors employ "deconstructive" metafictional strategies in order to demonstrate language's—particularly fictional language's—inability to reflect or "imitate" empirical reality, and in doing so, to reveal the inherent instability of fictional texts.

In *Flaubert's Parrot* metafictional elements assume a variety of forms: intertextuality, literary criticism, metaleptical intrusions, and parody. For example, in chapter seven, "Cross Channel," Braithwaite questions Flaubert's aesthetic of authorial impersonality:

> The author in his book must be like God in his universe, everywhere present and nowhere visible. Of course, this has been keenly misread in our century. Look at Sartre and Camus. God is dead, they told us, and therefore so is the God-like novelist. Omniscience is impossible, man's knowledge is partial, therefore the novel itself must be partial. That sounds not just splendid, but logical as well. But is it either? The novel, after all, didn't arise when belief in God arose; nor for that matter, is there much correlation between those novelists who believed most strongly in the omniscient narrator and those who believed most strongly in the omniscient creator. . . . More to the point, the assumed divinity of the nineteenth century novelist was only ever a technical device; and the partiality is just as much a ploy. (91)

Ironically, Braithwaite (whose own "story," it must be noted, ends "inconclusively" after a series of digressions and hesitations) then inveighs against all those contemporary novels, such as Fowles' *The French Lieutenant's Woman*, which provide readers with multiple endings:

> When the writer provides two different endings to his novel (why two? Why not a hundred?), does the reader seriously imagine he is being 'offered a choice' and that the work is reflecting life's variable outcomes? Such a 'choice' is never real, because the reader is obliged to consume both endings. . . . The novel with two endings doesn't reproduce this reality; it merely takes us down two diverging paths. It's a form of cubism, I suppose, but let's not deceive ourselves about the artifice involved. (91)

To the novelist who "truly wanted to simulate the delta of life's possibilities," Braithwaite proposes the following model: books which conclude with sealed envelopes containing different endings—"Traditional Happy Ending," "Traditional Unhappy Ending," "Traditional Half and Half Ending," "Deus Ex Machina," "Modernist Arbitrary Ending," etc.—from which the reader would be allowed to choose only one.

In another wry aside, Braithwaite comments on contemporary fiction's "hesitating narrator," and in so doing ironically calls attention to his own favorite narrative technique:

> When a contemporary narrator hesitates, claims uncertainty, misunderstands, plays games and falls into error, does the reader in fact conclude that reality is being more authentically rendered? . . . . As for the hesitating narrator—look I'm afraid you've run into one right now. It must be because I'm English. You'd guessed that, at least—that I'm English? I. . . I. . .Look at that seagull up there. I hadn't spotted him before. Slipstreaming away, waiting for the bits of gristle from the sandwiches. Listen, I hope you won't think this rude, but I really must take a turn on deck; it's becoming quite stuffy in the bar here. . . . Besides, I'm going to the lavatory first. I can't have you following me in there, peering around from the next stall. . . . I apologise, I didn't mean that. . . . Oh, and one last word. The cheese shop in the Grande Rue: don't miss it. I think the name's Leroux. I suggest you get a Brillat-Savarin. . . . That is, if you like cheese . . . . (92–93)

Of course, while the intrusive author/narrator has been a common feature of the novel since its inception, its function in 18th and 19th century fiction is not, strictly speaking, "metafictional." According to Patricia Waugh, whereas the use of this device in the early novel tended to blend smoothly with the "story," and thus preserve the illusion of reality, the postmodernist intrusive author/narrator serves to expose the text's artifice by making the reader aware of the conflicting ontological levels involved in fictional representation:

> . . . although Fielding, Trollope, and George Eliot, for example, often 'break the frame' of their novels, they are by no means self-conscious novelists in the sense in which the term has been discussed here. Although the intrusive commentary of nineteenth-century fiction may at times be metalingual (referrring to fictional codes themselves), it functions mainly to aid the readerly concretization of the world of

the book by forming a bridge between the historical and the fictional worlds. It suggests that the one is merely a continuation of the other, and it is thus not metafictional.

In *Adam Bede* (1859), . . . , George Eliot destroys the illusion of Hayslope's self-containedness by continually intruding moralistic commentary, interpretation and appeals to the reader. However, such intrusions do in fact reinforce the connection between the real and the fictional world, reinforce the reader's sense that one is a continuation of the other. In metafictional texts such intrusions expose the ontological distinctness of the real and fictional world, expose the literary conventions that disguise this distinctness. (31–32)

Moreover, the peculiar configurations of biographical material in *Flaubert's Parrot* reveal Barnes' distinctively postmodernist sense of irony and coincidence, as well as his fascination with the ways in which art, despite Flaubert's insistence to the contrary, mingles with reality. Here, for instance, is how Barnes introduces Eleanor Marx, daughter of Karl Marx and first English translator of *Madame Bovary*:

E1 was born in 1855.
E2 was partly born in 1855.
E1 had an unclouded childhood but emerged into adulthood inclined to nervous crisis.
E2 had an unclouded childhood but emerged into adulthood inclined to nervous crisis.
E1 led a life of sexual irregularity in the eyes of right-thinking people.
E2 led a life of sexual irregularity in the eyes of right-thinking people.
E1 imagined herself to be in financial difficulties.
E2 knew herself to be in financial difficulties.
E1 committed suicide by swallowing prussic acid.
E2 committed suicide by swallowing arsenic.
E1 is Eleanor Marx.
E2 is Madame Bovary (199–200)

As was noted earlier, *Flaubert's Parrot* derives much of its post-modernist character from the ways in which Barnes uses metafictional techniques to foreground the various figural and narrative structures which constitute his novel's "fictiveness." A good example of this is the passage quoted above, where Barnes attempts to establish "ontological" parallels between a historical figure, Eleanor Marx, and a fictional character, Emma Bovary. Throughout, Braithwaite makes references to real people and places: Flaubert, Enid Starkie, Christopher Ricks, Rouen, and Croisset. In historiographic metafiction, the introduction of historical figures serves to widen the "ontological" gap between fiction and reality. According to Patricia Waugh, "Metafictional texts which introduce real peope and events expose not only the illusion of verisimilar writing but also that of historical writing itself" (106). As Both Linda Hutcheon and Alison Lee observe, however, post- modernism's use of "real people" is quite different from that of traditional historical fiction.

> In the nineteenth century novel, real people, places, and events were included or alluded to in order to convince the reader of the "truth" of the fictional ones. In historiographic metafiction, however, instead of historical characters and events proving the truth of the fiction, they point to the indeterminacy of historical knowledge. (Lee 52)

This is most certainly true in the case of *Flaubert's Parrot*, where the introduction of real people, far from facilitating historical understanding, serves merely to problematize Braithwaite's apparent confidence in the ability of factual documentation to reveal truth.

Unlike more conventional "lives" of Flaubert (or of any other individual for that matter)—such as those by Enid Starkie and Herbert Lottman—which reveal subject mainly through linear documentary exposition, Barnes' "biography" is interwoven with fictional narrative; the life of Flaubert unfolds in fits and starts, zig-zagging tentatively through the mind of Barnes' main character and occasional first-person narrator. According to one commentator,

> Conventional biography insists that subject comprehension rises out of encyclopedic narration, that a sequential rendering of an entire data pool . . . comes nearest to replication of a subject. Braithwaite avoids this form of representation, limiting himself to narratives about his own life and to a fabulous construction of 'Louise Colet's' version. (White 114)

Barnes' combative polemicism, his humorous forays into literary criticism—especially his attacks on Enid Starkie and Jean-Paul Sartre—impart further metafictional dimensions to his novel. One such diatribe appears in Chapter Six, "Emma Bovary's Eye," in which Barnes pits his narrator against the dreadnought of academic criticism. The target of his attack in this instance is the distinguished French literary scholar and critic, Enid Starkie, whose two-volume biography of Flaubert contains the following comment:

> Flaubert does not build up his characters, as did Balzac, through objective, external description; in fact, so careless is he of their outward appearance that on one occasion he gives Emma brown eyes (14); on another deep black eyes (15); and on another blue eyes (16). (Barnes 74)

For Braithwaite the preceding comment apparently reflects the kind of pedantic narrow-mindedness and inaccuracy which plagues much modern "institutionalized" literary criticism. What Professor Starkie's remarks fail to consider, Braithwaite argues, is Flaubert's right as an artist to take certain liberties with his subject—his right to use any means at his disposal to render character, setting, and narrative incident—so long as those means do not compromise the truthfulness of his vision. As Braithwaite implies, Emma's changing eye colors do not result from a lapse on Flaubert's part (as Professor Starkie seems to suggest) but rather from Emma's varying moods and from the way in which light happens to strike her eyes in different settings. Thus, Emma's "inconsistent" eye coloring represents one aspect of Flaubert's vision of her character.

In the same chapter, Braithwaite expresses his perturbation with "critics who treat fiction as documentary history" (Lee 2):

> I'll remember instead another lecture I once attended. . . . It was given by a professor from Cambridge, Christopher Ricks, and it was a very shiny performance. His bald head was shiny; his black shoes were shiny; and his lecture was very shiny indeed. Its theme was Mistakes in Literature and Whether They Matter. Yevtushenko, for example, apparently made a howler in one of his poems about the American nightingale. Pushkin was quite wrong about the sort of military dress worn at balls. John Wain was wrong about the Hiroshima pilot. Nabokov was wrong—rather surprising this—about the phonetics of the name Lolita. There were other examples: Coleridge, Yeats and Browning were some of those caught not knowing a hawk from a handsaw, or not even knowing what a hand-saw was in the first place. (76)

Braithwaite's vexation is ironical given his own penchant for documenting biographical facts about the life of Flaubert, a writer who, as Braithwaite himself concedes, "disdainfully forbade posterity to take any personal interest in . . ." (16). Indeed, as Alison Lee explains, *Flaubert's Parrot*'s very enactment of the problematic relation of art to life is embodied in the contradictions which Braithwaite exhibits in his respective roles as character and narrator. As "character," Lee argues, Braithwaite believes that the accumulation of biographical facts will lead to a greater understanding of Flaubert's life, and that this, in turn, will allow him to achieve a fuller appreciation of Flaubert's fiction. As "character," then, Braithwaite affirms realism's faith in the "veracity of the facts" (Lee, 3). As "narrator," however, Braithwaite's obtrusive digressiveness tends to subvert the very realism he places such stock in as "character." According to Lee:

> as a character Braithwaite is obsessed by concerns we might associate with Realist reading—detail, authority, intention, reference—as a narrator, he constantly undermines his own obsessions. In this mode he is self-conscious and intrusive.

He offers the reader advice on cheese, dictates types of novels which should and should not be written. . . . And he forbids the reader to pursue him. . . . He offers parodic imitations of Flaubert's *Dictionnaire des idees recues*, of chronologies of Flaubert's life, . . . and even an examination paper. Each of these is, to some extent, a parrot, a way of imitating Flaubert in the hope that the imitation will reflect the truth. (38-39)

Indeed, it might be argued that the postmodern character of *Flaubert's Parrot* derives, in part, from just this very intrusiveness—from the irony of using a highly visible narrator in a novel which purports to recount certain biographical facts about Gustave Flaubert, the famous French author whose own act of dispensing with the visible, or "intrusive," narrator fathered the modern novel. Indeed, the book's opening image—that of a group of North African youths playing *boules* beneath a crumbling statue of Flaubert—ironically reflects the "master's" doctrine of authorial self-effacement. In accordance with Flaubert's precept that the aesthetic object is everything, the artist nothing, authorial presence will be "refined out of existence." The artist's identity, like the disintegrating statue which French officials try desperately to restore, fades away. As Barnes' narrator tells us,

I begin with the statue, because that's where I began the whole project. Why does the writing make us chase the writer? Why can't we leave well enough alone? Why aren't the books enough? Flaubert wanted them to be: few writers believed more in the objectivity of the written text and the insignificance of the writer's personality; yet still we disobediently pursue. . . . Don't we believe the words enough? (2-3)

What *Flaubert's Parrot* reveals, however, is that for Barnes' chatty, digressive narrator, "the books" and "the words" are clearly not enough, and Braithwaite's chief activity throughout the novel will be to ferret out as many details about Flaubert's "personality" as he can—in part to dispel various rumors and misconceptions about the French writer's life; in part to demonstrate the enormous difficulties inherent in writing biography, and in part to indulge his own curiosity. However, like Bouvard and Pecuchet's "life" of the Duc d'Angouleme (*Bouvard and Pecuchet* is another intertext in *Flaubert's Parrot*), Braithwaite's "biography" of Flaubert becomes an encyclopedic collection of disparate fragments—relics, anecdotal bric-a-brac—which resist coherent integration. Occasionally, his investigation leads him into areas which seem at best only tangentially related to Flaubert's life. Indeed, Braithwaite's attention to minutiae becomes so absorbing that after reading about how Flaubert had once "watched the sun go down over the seas and declared that it resembled a large disc of redcurrat jam," he consults a grocer's company to find out if the modern version of this jam would be the same color as it was in 1853. When the grocer assures Braithwaite that it would, the latter writes, "So at least that's all right: now we can go ahead and confidently imagine the sunset" (93).

In another "digression," Braithwaite compiles a "bestiary," a list of all the animals—including the bear, the camel, the sheep, the parrot, and the dog—that Flaubert had ever seen, imagined, delighted in, dined with, fictionalized, and compared himself to. This chapter—yet one more piece in Braithwaite's collage-like recreation of Flaubert—proves to be another instance of the narrator's "parrotry," since it contains excerpts from Flaubert's journals and letters. "I am a bear," Flaubert ("Flaubear") writes in one entry, "and I want to stay a bear in my den, in my lair, in my skin, in my old bear's skin; I want to live quietly, far away from the bourgeois and the bourgeoises" (44). Under "Camel," Flaubert notes: "I am, in both my physical and my mental activity, like the dromedary, which is very hard to get going and very hard, once it is going, to stop; continuity is what I need, whether of rest or of motion" (51). And in the "Parrot" section, Flaubert describes the differences between "pride" and "vanity": "Pride is a wild beast which lives in caves and roams the desert; Vanity, on the other hand, is a parrot which hops from branch to branch and chatters away in full view" (56).

In Chapter 8, "The Train-Spotter's Guide to Flaubert," we learn that the French author despised the railroad, even though it helped expedite his assignations with Louise Colet. Since Louise lived in Paris and Gustave lived in Rouen, the two lovers frequently met at Mantes, a village located equidistantly between the two cities. The invention of the train made it possible to reduce traveling time for each of the lovers from one day to two hours. Halfway through the chapter, however, Braithwaite interrupts his discourse on the railroad's role in Flaubert's life to inform us that he himself had recently traveled the same line from Rouen to Mantes, retracing, and in a sense "parroting," Flaubert's journey (the fact that Lousie Colet was cuckolding her husband during her trysts with Flaubert adds an ironical twist to the narrator's excursion to Mantes). As Patti White observes:

> Braithwaite assembles, collates, and, eventually, fabricates data that, in the variety of their patterns and configurations, suggest a potentially comprehensive discovery or representation of Flaubert. However, the informational models encoding Flaubert in Braithwaite's final document valorize fragmentation as a means of representation, actualizing in their structures the arbitrary and incomplete nature of personal historiography. (113)

White further argues that the "mosaic effect" of Braithwaite's "biography" "pushes it toward the status of documentary museum, a relationally randomized collection of disparate items placed together under an assumption that spatial contiguity enacts conceptual contiguity, and that subject comprehension can rise up out of datic conglomeration" (114). In the end, Braithwaite's meticulous collection of evidence will fail to produce a comprehensive understanding of Flaubert.

Braithwaite's search for the authentic stuffed parrot which had once perched itself so "irritatingly" on Flaubert's writing table while the latter composed "A Simple Heart" will force Barnes' narrator to confront several compelling questions about the nature of truth, the lessons of the past, and the relationship between art and reality: how, for example, do we arrive at truth? Can truth be known at all? How reliable is the past in helping us ascertain truth? Does the kind of factual documentation we normally encounter in biographical works, particularly literary biographies, accurately reflect the truth about their subjects' lives? Does truth reside merely in the documentation of factual data? Can biography be distinguished from fiction?

Woven through the novel like a lietmotif, Braithwaite's reflections on the past and its relation to truth assume various metaphorical guises: a greased pig, an ambulance, a receding coastline—all of which underscore the novel's very enactment of the indeterminacy of historical meaning.

> How do we seize the past? Can we ever do so? When I was a medical student some prankster at an end-of-term dance released into the hall a piglet which had been smeared with grease. It squirmed between legs, evaded capture, squealed a lot. People fell over trying to grasp it, and were made to look ridiculous in the process. The past often seems to behave like that greased piglet. (5)
>
> Parked near the hospital was a large white Peugeot hatchback: it was painted with blue stars, a telephone number and the words AMBULANCE FLAUBERT. The writer as healer? Unlikely. I remembered George Sand's matronly rebuke to her younger colleague: 'You produce desolation,' she said, 'and I produce consolation.' The Peugeot should have been named AMBULANCE GEORGE SAND. (5)
>
> *Flaubert's Parrot* Do you want art to be a healer? Send for the AMBULANCE GEORGE SAND. Do you want art to tell the truth? Send for the AMBULANCE FLAUBERT: though don't be surprised, when it arrives, if it runs over your legs. (151)
>
> The past is a distant, receding coastline, and we are all in the same boat. Along the stern rail there is a line of telescopes; each brings the shore into focus at a given distance. If the boat is becalmed, one of the telescopes will be in continual

use; it will seem to tell the whole truth. But this is an illusion; and as the boat sets off again, we return to our normal activity: scurrying from one telescope to another, seeing the sharpness fade in one, waiting for the blur to clear in another. And when the blur does clear, we imagine that we have made it do so all by ourselves. (107)

As it happens, biographical "histories" prove to be no less elusive than social, cultural, or political histories. This is the apparent theme of chapter two. The chapter is divided into three sections, the first two of which contain chronologies of important events in Flaubert's life, while the final section offers a chronology of Flaubert's reflections on various literary and philosophical subjects.

Comprising section one, the first chronology highlights the types of "objective" historical facts traditionally appended to "student" or annotated college editions of a writer's works: the more or less standard outline of important events in the life of the author, including year of birth, formal education, beginnings of friendships and/or literary associations, dates of various publications, and the year of the writer's death. However, as if to counterbalance the affirmative tone of section one, which deals mainly with positive, triumphant events in Flaubert's life, the second chronology, although again presented "objectively," provides the kind of biographical material not traditionally included in standard annotated editions of literary texts. The entries in this second section enumerate the deaths of Flaubert's friends and family members, as well as periods in the writer's life in which Flaubert experienced some kind of physical or emotional crisis. Thus, whereas section one had focused on triumphs and successes, section two highlights tragedy and failure, revealing darker aspects of Flaubert's life.

By juxtaposing a chronology which enumerates Flaubert's personal, literary, and social "triumphs" with one which outlines his "failures" and "crises," Barnes reveals the deficiencies inherent in biographical "sketches" of this type. Cross-referencing entries from the first two chronologies shows how easy it is to interpret the same event in different ways:

1836   (first chronology)—[Flaubert] meets Elisa Schlesinger, wife of a German music publisher, in Trouville, and conceives an 'enormous' passion for her. This passion illuminates the rest of his adolescence. She treats him with great kindness and affection; they remain in touch for the next forty years. Looking back, he is relieved she didn't return his passion: 'Happiness is like a pox. Catch it too soon and it wrecks your constitution.'

1836	(corresponding entry in second chronology)—The start of a hopeless, obsessive passion for Elisa Schlesinger which cauterises his heart and renders him incapable of ever fully loving another woman. Looking back, he records: 'Each of us possesses in his heart a royal chamber. I have bricked mine up.'
1844	(first chronology)—Gustave's first epileptic attack puts an end to legal studies in Paris and confines him to the new family house at Croisset. Abandoning the law, however, causes little pain, and since his confinement brings both the solitude and the stable base needed for a life of writing, the attack proves beneficial in the long run.
1844	(corresponding entry in second chronology)—Shattering first attack of epilepsy; others are to follow. 'Each attack,' Gustave writes later, 'was like a haemorhage of the nervous system. . . . It was a snatching away of the soul from the body, excruciating.' He is bled, given pills and infusions, put on a special diet, forbidden alcohol and tobacco; a regime of strict confinement and maternal care is necessary if he is not to claim his place at the cemetery. . . . For all but the last eight years of his life, Mme Flaubert watches suffocatingly over his welfare and censors his travel plans. Gradually over the decades, her frailty overtakes his: by the time he has almost ceased to be a worry to her, she has become a burden to him.
1851–57	(first chronology)—The writing, publication, trial, and triumphant acquittal of *Madame Bovary*. A *succes de scandale*, praised by authors as diverse as Lamartine, Sainte-Beuve and Baudelaire. In 1846, doubting his ability ever to write anything worth publishing, Gustave had announced, 'If I do make an appearance, one day, it will be in full armour.' Now his breastplate dazzles and his lance is everywhere. . . . After 1857, literary success leads to social success: Flaubert is seen more in Paris.
1851–57	(corresponding entry in second chronology)—*Madame Bovary*. The composition is painful—'Writing this book I am like a man playing the piano with lead balls attached to his knuckles'— and the prosecution frightening. In later years Flaubert comes to resent the insistent fame of his masterpiece, which makes others see him as a one-book author. He tells DuCamp that if ever he had a stroke of good luck on the bourse he would buy

	up 'at any cost' all copies of *Madame Bovary* in circulation: 'I should throw them into the fire, and never hear of them again.'
1880	(first chronology)—Full of honour, widely loved and still working hard to the end, Gustave Flaubert dies at Croisset.
1880	(corresponding entry in second chronology)—Impoverished, lonely and exhausted, Gustave Flaubert dies. . . . After the funeral a group of mourners, including the poets Francois Coppee and Theodore de Banville, have dinner in Rouen to honour the departed writer. They discover, on sitting down to table, that they are thirteen. The superstitious Banville insists that another guest be found, and Gautier's son-in-law, Emile Bergerat, is sent to scour the streets. He returns with a private on leave. The soldier has never heard of Flaubert, but is longing to meet Coppee. (16–25)

The final section of chapter two is a chronology of Flaubert's observations on such topics as love, sexuality, aesthetics, fiction, and cultural affairs. Written in the form of excerpts from letters and notebooks, these entries, many of which have a pungency reminiscent of Le Rochefoucauld's "Maxims," allow us to glimpse various moments in Flaubert's inner life, thus counterpointing the "objective" biographical material in the first two chronologies:

1852–	As you get older, the heart sheds its leaves like a tree. You cannot hold out against certain winds. Each day tears away a few more leaves; and then there are the storms which break off several branches at one go. And while nature's greenery grows back again in the spring, that of the heart never grows back.
1852–	What an awful thing life is, isn't it? It's like soup with lots of hairs floating on the surface. You have to eat it nevertheless.
1852–	I love my work with a frantic and perverted love, as an ascetic loves the hair-shirt which scratches his belly.
1854–	You ask for love, you complain that I don't send you flowers? Flowers indeed! If that's what you want, find yourself some wet-eared boy stuffed with fine manners and all the right ideas. I'm like the tiger, which has bristles of hair at the end of his cock, with which he lacerates the female.
1857–	Books aren't made in the way babies are: they are made like pyramids. There's some long-pondered plan, and then great

	blocks of stone are placed one on top of the other, and it's back-breaking, sweaty, time-consuming work. And all to no purpose! It just stands like that in the desert! But it towers over it prodigiously. Jackals piss at the base of it, and the bourgeois clamber to the top of it, etc. Continue this comparison.
1872—	Never have things of the spirit counted for so little. Never has hatred for everything been so manifest—disdain for beauty, execration of literature. I have always tried to live in an ivory tower, but a tide of shit is beating at its walls, threatening to undermine it.

"Life," in the final analysis, can never be fully articulated by the "parrotry" of biographical exposition. Rather, the writer's mind and soul find expression chiefly in his or her writings. Any biographical reconstruction of a writer's life will of necessity be fragmentary and incomplete; moreover, insofar as the "Life" will be shaped by the biographer's racial, social, and sexual biases, it will fail to render its subject truthfully. The selection (what kind of material gets put in and what kind gets left out) and interpretation of biographical data always reflect the biographer's prejudices. As Braithwaite points out:

> You can define a net in one of two ways, depending on your point of view. Normally, you would say that it is a meshed instrument designed to catch fish. But you could, with no great injury to logic, reverse the image and define a net as a jocular lexicographer once did: he called it a collection of holes tied together with string.
> You can do the same with a biography. The trawling nets fill, then the biographer hauls it in, sorts, throws back, stores, fillets, and sells. Yet consider what he doesn't catch: there is always far more of that . . . think of everything that got away, that fled with the last death-bed exhalation of the biographee. (31)

Flaubert's Parrot leaves us, finally, with a feeling that truth is unattainable and the past inaccessible—but not, however, before taking us on an extended tour of the narrator's life, Flaubert's life, and the life of fiction. These themes are developed through the interweaving of two main narrative strands, both of which intricately involve the lives of the narrator, the narrator's wife, Flaubert, and two of Flaubert's most famous fictional characters. The unfolding narrative reveals a parallel development between Braithwaite's attempts to piece together the life of Flaubert and his struggle to come to terms with his wife's death—and ultimately with the meaning of his own life. What soon becomes clear is that Braithwaite's endeavor to understand all of this—the meaning of his life, his marriage, and his wife's "suicide"—recapitulates the literary biographer's own struggle to discover truths about his or her subject. As one commentator observes:

> Braithwaite's document slides toward self-totalization even as it works to encircle Flaubert, and his narrative persona necessarily fabulates Flaubert as much as the Colet version does.
>
> A fragmentary and incomplete Braithwaite autobiography nests within his fragmented biography of Flaubert. (White 114)

This intermingling of fictional and historical characters can be observed in Chapter Ten, "The Case Against," which finds Braithwaite reflecting briefly on the causes of his "failed" marriage before launching into a discussion of various charges that have been levelled against Flaubert's "personality" over the years by readers and critics. In the hope of arriving at some kind of understanding of his relationship with his wife and the problems which led to their "estrangement," Braithwaite introduces the chapter by posing the question: "What makes us want to know the worst?" Is it simply that we tire of knowing the best? Does our need to dredge up the "bad" betray some defect in human nature? For Braithwaite, wanting to know the worst about his wife sprang from a love which he characterizes as total and honest. By contrast, he implies, his wife's rather facile presumptions about his "good nature"—his lack of bad qualities—reflect her own emotional shortcomings. "I loved Ellen," Braithwaite tells us

> . . . and I wanted to know the worst. I never provoked her; I was cautious and defensive, as is my habit; I didn't even ask questions; but I wanted to know the worst. Ellen never returned this caress. She was fond of me—she would automatically agree, as if the matter weren't worth discussing, that she loved me—but she unquestioningly believed the best about me. That's the difference. She didn't ever search for that sliding panel which opens the secret chamber of the heart, the chamber where memory and corpses are kept. . . . That's the real distinction between people: not between those who have secrets and those who don't, but between those who want to know everything and those who don't. This search is a sign of love, I maintain. (138–139)

Braithwaite then applies this principle to writers and books, arguing that when an individual "loves" a writer (as he himself apparently admires Flaubert), he will immerse himself in the writer's life:

> It's similar with books. . . . If you quite enjoy a writer's work, if you turn the page approvingly yet don't mind being interrupted, then you tend to like the author unthinkingly. Good chap, you assume. Sound fellow. They say he strangled an entire pack of Wolf Cubs and fed their bodies to a school of carp? Oh no, I'm sure he didn't: sound fellow, good chap. But if you love a writer, if you depend

upon the drip-feed of his intelligence, if you want to pursue him and find him—despite edicts to the contrary—then it's impossible to know too much. You seek the vice as well. (139)

The passage quoted immediately above serves as a bridge between Braithwaite's reflections on marriage and his "defense" of Flaubert's moral and aesthetic visions, visions which he suggests have been traduced by pedantry and parochialism.

Flaubert's Parrot serves up many ironical parallels between the life of its narrator and several key events in Flaubert's masterpiece of irony, *Madame Bovary*. Like Charles Bovary, for instance, Geoffrey Braithwaite is a doctor who, although monogamous himself, is married to an adulterous woman. What is more, Braithwaite's wife, like that of his fictional counterpart, commits suicide. As one critic writes: "Geoffrey . . . knows that he and his wife have already been written, but he strives for a Flaubertian detachment, objectivity and impersonality, struggling at all odds to avoid becoming Flaubert's 'parrot', yet another husband merely repeating the pattern of Charles Bovary" (Higdon 180). For Braithwaite, "Flaubert's novels are the key to Flaubert, and Flaubert, who proved himself in *Madame Bovary* to be the master of creative adultery, is the key to unlocking the mysteries of his own troubles with the wandering affections of his wife" (Lee 37).

The chief effect of these manipulations—an impression of life intersecting with art—presupposes an "ontological" distinction between the "real" lives of Geoffrey Braithwaite and his wife on the one hand and the "fictional" lives of Charles and Emma Bovary on the other. If Barnes' intention is to explore ways in which art and life occasionally merge with one another, then his immediate problem becomes that of creating the illusion of Braithwaite's "reality." Barnes must impart the impression that Braithwaite's life is somehow more "real" than that of Flaubert's "fictional" doctor, notwithstanding the fact that both figures are "characters" in a novel by Julian Barnes. He achieves this, in part, by allowing Braithwaite to call attention to his role as narrator—to the fact that his words constitute a "readable" text—a narrative ploy which lends legitimacy to the impression that Braithwaite has an autonomous reality, a life outside the fictional world of the text he narrates. Of course, this illusion of Braithwaite's separate, detachable "reality" is negated the moment he acts as the central narrator in Julian Barnes' novel. Braithwaite's "reality" co-extends merely with his function as "narrator" and "character."

Compounding the irony, of course, is Braithwaite's very fascination with the French novelist who created Charles and Emma Bovary, characters whose own fictional lives, as we have seen, parallel the life of Barnes' narrator. That Braithwaite should choose to admire Flaubert, "the master of creative adultery," is one of the book's supreme ironies. Add to this the fact that Barnes' "biographical" excursion (via his narrator) into the real life of Gustave Flaubert—a writer deeply concerned with the relationship between fiction and reality—takes place within the fictional world of Geoffrey Braithwaite, and what we are left with is a novel whose narrative structure, like those of *Don Quixote* and *Tristram Shandy*, incorporates several levels of fictional "reality."

In its consistent expropriation of other literary genres, as well as in its treatment of the very problem which Flaubert devoted his entire life to— the problem of making novels—*Flaubert's Parrot* exemplifies contemporary fiction's so-called "self-consciousness" or "self-reflexivity." The result is a book which combines humor, sensitivity, and absorbing insights not only into the processes of literary creation but also into the complexities of 20th century man's pursuit of truth.

Chapter 3

A History of the World in 10 1/2 Chapters

Barnes' fourth novel, *A History of the World in 10 1/2 Chapters*, exemplifies several of the major tendencies of postmodernist historical fiction. Like the fictions of Robert Coover, Salman Rushdie, E.L. Doctorow, and John Fowles, Barnes' novel reveals how the process of narrativization itself problematizes not only the nature of historical discourse but also the relationship between history and fiction. Perhaps his most ambitious venture into "historical" fiction to date, *A History of the World in 10 1/2 Chapters* is at once a narrative of man's capacity to inflict cruelty on his fellow man (as well as on the natural world) and, to a lesser extent, an affirmation of the human spirit's tenacious will to survive such cruelty.

To readers already familiar with postmodernist narrative strategies, especially with those which play havoc with such traditional literary elements as closure and narrative linearity—including flashback, flashforward (a technique used with extraordinary adroitness in Salman Rushdie's *Midnight's Children* and Martin Amis' *London Fields*), retrospective narration, and montaging, it should come as little surprise that the fourteen stories which comprise *A History of The World in 10 1/2 Chapters* are not arranged in any kind of chronological sequence, even though such "tampering" might seem, initially, at odds with a text whose title promises "A History of the World." Nor should it seem especially surprising to those intitiated in the duplicities of contemporary "historiographic" fiction (particularly that variety which Linda Hutcheon and Patricia Waugh have identified as "Historiographic Metafiction") that several of the "historical events" which Barnes records in his book have no basis in historical fact whatsoever, or that Barnes should feel free at times to take certain liberties with those events which do.

However, although on the surface its stories seem to be unconnected and thus give the book the impression of being a loosely organized collection of vignettes, *A History of the World in 10 1/2 Chapters* is actually held together by a number of interlocking motifs and recurrent images, the principal ones being water and the Biblical Flood Myth. Seven of the fourteen stories—"Stowaway," "The Visitors," "The Survivor," "Upstream," "Shipwreck," and two tales from a chapter entitled "Three Simple Stories"—take place at sea, either entirely or in part ("Upstream" is actually set on a river in South America). The other seven stories have off-water settings (the final chapter takes place in Heaven). However, all the stories in the book, including those which do not take place at sea, contain references to Noah and the Flood Myth. Thus, whereas the temporal randomness of the text serves to deconstruct any sense of a coherently unfolding historical totality, its underlying thematic and tropological connections reveal how history lumbers forward in endless variations on a theme.

The connective patterns which make *A History*'s underlying structural cohesion possible are established in the first chapter, "Stowaway." Narrated by a woodworm (termite?) which, together with six other members of its species, has managed to board Noah's Ark undetected (woodworm were not included on the ship's original passenger list, making clandestine embarkation necessary), "Stowaway" contains all of the book's central motifs: The Noah story (with its water imagery, pairs of animals, separation of animals into "clean" and "unclean" types, and bitumen), reindeer, woodworm, ships being lost at sea/shipwrecked, Mt. Ararat, and *xestobium rufo villosum*—a curious species of insect which announces its mating instincts by rapping its head against walls and other solid objects.

"Stowaway" retells the Flood Myth from the woodworm's vantage point, and the portrait of Noah which emerges from this particular narrator's "eye-witness" account debunks that which inhabits both sacred text and the popular imagination:

> I don't know how best to break this to you, but Noah was not a nice man. I realize this idea is embarrassing, since you are all descended from him; still, there it is. He was a monster, a puffed-up patriarch who spent half his day grovelling to his God and the other half taking it out on us. (12)

Instead of a kindly, venerable old patriarch, what we read about is an "old rogue with a drink problem who was already into his seventh century of life" (8), and who ran his ark like a prison ship. Barnes' narrator describes Noah as a cruel, drunken, and incompetent sea captain who, along with other members of his family, delights in tormenting the animals which have been placed in his charge.

As if to disabuse us of our quaint notions of the Flood Myth, the narrator insists that man's "official" Biblical account of Noah's mission is riddled with errors and inconsistencies, and that the actual event departs dramatically from those "nursery versions in painted wood which you might have played with as a child—all happy couples peering merrily over the rail from the comfort of their well-scrubbed stalls" (3). For one thing—the narrator informs us—Noah's Ark was not one ship, but a whole flotilla (some 8 vessels in all), and several of the ships, including one that was apparently reserved for sexual diversions, were lost at sea, and with them many species of animal life. Moreover, one of the ill-fated vessels was captained by Noah's fourth and youngest son, Varardi, whose youthfulness, strength, cheerful disposition, and popularity with many of the animals did little to endear him to the rest of his family—a possible explanation, the narrator hints, for Varardi's mysterious omission from *Genesis*:

> [Varadi] . . . had a sense of humor—or at least he laughed a lot, which is usually proof enough for your species. Yes, Varadi was always cheerful. He could be seen strutting the quarterdeck with a parrot on each shoulder; he would slap the quadrupeds affectionately on the rump, which they acknowledged with an appreciative bellow; and it was said that his ark was run on much less tyrannical lines than the others. But there you are: one morning we woke to find that Varadi's ship had vanished from the horizon, taking with it one-fifth of the animal kingdom. . . . Varadi's elder brothers blamed poor navigation; they said Varadi had spent far too much time fraternizing with the beasts; they even hinted that God might have been punishing him for some obscure offense committed when he was a child of eighty-five. But whatever the truth behind Varadi's disappearance, it was a severe loss to your species. His genes would have helped you a great deal. (6)

Another error that the narrator hastens to correct concerns the actual time span of the Flood.

> It rained forty days and forty nights? Well, naturally it didn't—that would have been no more than a routine English summer. No, it rained for about a year and a half, by my reckoning. And the waters were upon the earth for a hundred and fifty days? Bump that to about four years. And so on. Your species has always been hopeless about dates. I put it down to your quaint obsession with multiples of seven. (5)

What is more, living conditions aboard ship were far from satisfactory. After all, the Flood voyage was not, in the words of the narrator, "some Mediterranean cruise on which [the animals] played langorous roulette and everyone dressed for dinner" (3). Not only was hygiene a constant problem, but the animals were daily subjected to the taunts and repressive disciplinary actions of Noah and his family. For one thing, sick animals were "ruthlessly dealt with. . . . A little bit of mange and you were over the side before you could stick your tongue out for inspection" (13). Other animals were punished for the slightest misdemeanors. Sexual misconduct, for instance, could call down the sternest reprisals, as in the case of the donkey, which was keel-hauled for mounting a mare. Many animals—including the basilisk, the griffon, the sphinx, and the hippogriff—were exterminated because of what the narrator describes as Noah's horror of cross-breeding. In some cases whole species were annihilated simply on the basis of their similarity to other species. The magisterial behemoth, for example, was rendered superfluous by virtue of its close resemblance to the elephant, upon which grounds it was ordered killed and sliced up into steaks.

Of course, food was a persistent concern of Noah's family throughout the voyage. As the narrator puts it, "What the hell do you think Noah and his family ate in the Ark? They ate us, of course" (13). This meant that in some instances seven members of certain species were taken on board, not just two. The additional five animals were designated as "clean," an apellation which at first served merely to arouse the indignation of those animals considered "unclean"—that is, until it became clear that being "'clean' meant that you could be eaten" (10). As for food shortages after the Flood, the narrator suspects that Noah had planned for just such a contingency well in advance:

> You're probably still thinking that Noah, for all his faults was basically some kind of early conservationist, that he collected the animals together because he didn't want them to die out, that he couldn't endure not seeing a giraffe ever again, that he was doing it for us. This wasn't the case at all. He got us together because his role model told him to, but also out of self-interest, even cynicism. He wanted to have something to eat after the Flood had subsided . . . most of us knew that in Noah's eyes we were just future dinners on two, four, or however many legs. If not now, then later; if not us, then our offspring. (22)

Sometimes, however, the killings appeared to be motivated by even baser instincts—like greed, envy, and revenge. For example, the carbuncle was eradicated when Ham's wife—a real shrew of a woman according to the narrator—decided that she wanted the pearl which was located, so she believed, in the animal's tiny cranium. After failing to find one in the male's head, she ordered the female's split open as well—with the same unfortunate result. Shortly afterwards, two simians were put to death when it was discovered that Ham's wife had given birth to a child whose eye and hair coloring bore a closer resemblance to that of the male simian (green eyes and red hair) than it did to that of either the child's mother or

Ham (both of whom had brown eyes and dark hair). However, as distressing as these events were to the narrator, none of the deaths aboard the Ark aroused as much sadness as that of the unicorn:

> Of course, there were the usual sordid rumours—that Ham's wife had been putting its horn to ignoble use—and the usual posthumous smear campaign by the authorities about the beast's character; but this only sickened us the more. The unavoidable fact is that Noah was jealous. We all looked up to the unicorn, and he couldn't stand it. Noah—what point is there in not telling you the truth?—was badtempered, smelly, unreliable, and cowardly. . . . Whereas the unicorn was strong, honest, fearless, impeccably groomed and a mariner who never knew a moment's queasiness. (16)

The narrator recalls how the unicorn once used his horn to prevent Ham's wife from falling overboard during a gale, and how, for that act of heroism, he was casseroled "one Embarkation Sunday."

Not surprisingly, the voyage also took a devastating emotional toll on many of the animals, and according to the narrator, the species which displayed the most visible signs of this was the reindeer, whose increasing restiveness aboard the Ark seemed to betoken a deeper, more far-reaching sense of doom:

> With the reindeer it was more complicated. They were always nervous, but it wasn't just fear of Noah, it was something deeper. You know how some of us animals have powers of foresight? . . . . Anyway . . . the reindeer were troubled with something deeper than Noah-angst, stranger than storm-nerves; something . . . long-term. They sweated up in their stalls, they whinnied neurotically in spells of oppressive heat; they kicked out at the gopher-wood partitions when there was no danger. . . . It was something beyond what we then knew. As if they were saying. You think this is the worst? Don't count on it. Still, whatever it was, even the reindeer couldn't be specific about it. Something distant, major . . . long term. (12–13)

When next we read about the reindeer (several chapters later in a story called "The Survivor"), we learn that they have been irradiated by fallout from the Chernobyl nuclear disaster, thus fulfilling their earlier undefined premonitions:

> At first the plan had been to bury the reindeer six feet down. It wasn't much of a news story, just an inch or two on the foreign page. The cloud had gone over where the reindeer grazed, poison had come down in the rain, the lichen became radioactive, the reindeer had eaten the lichen and got radioactive themselves . . . . Then cartoonists started making jokes about how the reindeer were so gleaming with radioactivity that Father Christmas didn't need headlights on his sleigh, and Rudolph the red-nosed reindeer had a very shiny nose because he came from Chernobyl. (85)

But although he attributes many of the animals' deaths and much of their emotional distress to Noah's defective moral character, it is not just the latter's character which the narrator impugns; he also questions some of God's actions. Calling Him an "oppressive role-model," the narrator goes so far as to suggest God's complicity in the atrocities aboard the Ark. After all, he asks, if it was man's sinful nature which provoked Divine retribution, why did the rest of the animal kingdom have to suffer? Furthermore, why, out of the whole human race, did God decide to spare the life of a man whose ethical values were certainly not above reproach? And it wasn't just Noah's brutal treatment of the animals that disturbed the narrator; on occasion old Noah was known to direct his rage at members of his own family: consider, for instance, what he did to his son Ham when the latter discovered his father's nakedness. And how about that much-celebrated covenant? God's final pact with Noah didn't have much in it for the animals. A rainbow, the narrator insists, is small compensation for the loss of the unicorn and the despair of the reindeer—all of which observations lead the narrator to the conclusion that God uses some rather crude intimidation methods to govern his universe.

The narrator's bewilderment leaves him with one overriding question: how could a man like Noah—a man who "spent half his day grovelling to his God and the other half taking it out on us"—have inspired such timeless and universal adulation? He attributes it mainly to mankind's proneness to a certain inflexibility of mind, to his way of distorting "truth" to fit his own prejudices and preconceived notions. Based on what he has observed aboard the Ark (as well as on what the various species of birds reported to him) the narrator concludes that man is not a fully evolved species. Unlike the so-called "lower" animals, which always know exactly what they are and where they stand in the chain of being, humans never seem to be satisfied with their "appointed" place, but instead go careening between absurd extremes of behavior, sometimes preferring tameness and other times wildness. Moreover, the narrator notes,

> You aren't too good with the truth either, your species. You keep forgetting things, or you pretend to. . . . I can see there might be a positive side to this wilful averting of the eye: ignoring the bad things makes it easier for you to carry on. But ignoring the bad things makes you end up believing that bad things never happen. You are always surprised by them. It surprises you that guns kill, that money corrupts, that snow falls in winter. Such naivete can be charming; alas, it can also be perilous. (29)

Then too there is man's habit of shifting the responsibility for failure onto someone or something else:

Blame someone else, that's always your first instinct. And if you can't blame someone else, then start claiming the problem isn't a problem anyway. Rewrite the rules, shift the goalposts. (29)

A case in point, argues the narrator, is Noah's alcoholism. Some biblical scholars have attempted to explain it away by blaming it on the goat. It was the goat, they insist, that taught Noah how to drink, just as it was the serpent that introduced man to sin. Still other scholars have labored over ways to reconcile the two contradictory images of Noah: God-fearing patriarch and belligerent drunk. How, they ask, could the Noah who commanded the Ark possibly be the same man who, after a night of drunken carousing, cursed one of his own sons? Their answer? "A simple case of mistaken identity": the Noah who lay naked in a drunken stupor was not the same man whom God had entrusted with the world's animal population. They were two entirely different men.

II

Barnes' next story, "The Visitors," which is loosely based on the 1981 Achille-Lauro highjacking incident, echoes the theme of "twos" introduced in the first chapter. Like "The Stowaway," "The Visitors" features "couples" at sea. This time, however, the couples are not the biblical animals of Noah's Ark but twentieth century men and women who are exploring ancient Minoan civilization aboard the *Santa Euphemia*, a Greek ship which cruises the Mediterranean, Adriatic, and Aegean Seas in search of the ruins and other artistic treasures of the Classical and pre-Classical worlds. The tour group itself consists of people from the United States, England, France, Italy, Sweden, and Japan. Their guide, an early middle-aged Englishman and media personality named Franklin Hughes, is best known as the host of a television series which presents lectures on the cultural history of ancient societies. When we first meet Franklin, he is standing on the main deck of the ship near the gangway, his right arm draped loosely around the shoulders of a young woman named Tricia Maitland, the latest in a long line of female "assistants" who accompany Franklin on his annual lecture tours. As they watch the passengers embarking in "obedient couples," Franklin, apparently reminded of Noah's Ark, observes, "The animals came in two by two."

Ten days into the voyage the *Santa Euphemia* is highjacked by an Arab terrorist group called "The Black Thunder" (the titular "visitors"). The group's purpose in seizing the ship is to secure the release of three of its comrades-in-arms who, owing chiefly to the intervention of the United

States, have been imprisoned in France and Italy. After herding the passengers into the ship's dining room "by twos," the terrorists then organize them into larger groups according to nationality—an action which prompts one of the hostages to quip "separating the clean from the unclean."

Because of both his position as tour leader and what the terrorist chief regards as Franklin's skill in public speaking, the latter is appointed liaison man, whose function is to transmit messages between the Black Thunder and the hostages. Fearing for Tricia's life, as well as for his own and for those of the other passengers, Franklin, who many months earlier had taken, owing to his mindfulness of Britain's tarnished political image around the world, the "prudent" step of acquiring an Irish passport, now advises Tricia, holder of English travel papers, to pose as his wife. This, he believes, will save Tricia's life by conferring Irish citizenship upon her (Franklin, here, is banking on the hope that the Arabs will be favorably disposed toward the citizens of those nations which, like Ireland, engage in "terrorist" acts).

Many hours later, when it becomes clear to the terrorists that the authorities with whom they have been negotiating will not meet their demands, they begin executing the passengers in pairs—two an hour. Before the killings actually begin, however, the terrorist chief orders Franklin to prepare, with some coaching from the Arab's second-in-command, a speech explaining to the hostages why it has become necessary to execute them. Appalled by this sudden turn of events, Franklin at first refuses, upbraiding the Arab leader for lacking the courage to do his "own dirty work." But Franklin's resolve falters when the terrorist chief hints that his refusal to speak may jeopardize the safety of Tricia. For Franklin, now left alone to ponder his options, the situation becomes unbearable. Fearing on the one hand that his refusal to speak on behalf of the terrorists may endanger Tricia's life and on the other that his co-operation may be misconstrued by the passengers as a desperate attempt to save his own life, Franklin finds himself in a dilemma which reminds him of a "psychology experiment" that he claims he had once had the misfortune of hosting on one of his television programs:

> One item in that show reported an experiment for measuring the point at which self-interest takes over from altruism. . . . The researchers had taken a female monkey who had recently given birth and put her in a special cage. The mother was still feeding and grooming her infant in a way presumably not too dissimilar from the maternal behavior of the experimenters' wives. Then they turned a switch and began heating up the metal floor of the monkey's cage. At first she jumped around in discomfort, then squealed a lot, then took to standing on alter-

nate legs, all the while holding her infant in her arms. The floor was made hotter, the monkey's pain more evident. At a certain point the heat from the floor became unbearable, and she was faced with a choice, . . . , between altruism and self-interest. She either had to suffer extreme pain and perhaps death to protect her offspring or else place her infant on the floor and stand on it to keep herself from harm. In every case, sooner or later, self-interest had triumphed over altruism. (52–53)

Should Franklin go the way of altruism and deliver the speech without regard for the way the other hostages will interpret his actions—in which case he saves Tricia from certain death? Or should he give in to the pressures of self-interest and refuse to speak—in which case he preserves the integrity of his public image? Suddenly mindful of the difference between monkeys and human beings, Franklin opts for altruism. After delivering his "lecture," he returns to his cabin, where, moments later, he hears the gunfire which signals that the executions have begun. The highjacking ends several hours later, when a team of American commandos storms the ship and kills most of the terrorists (the crossfire claims the lives of several of the hostages as well), including the leader and the second-in-command, the only two men who could have verified the "deal" Franklin had made with them in order to save his "wife's" life.

In part, "The Visitors" shapes itself around the interrelationship between history, rhetoric, and narrative. As a "lecturer" on history, Franklin likens himself to a story-teller who becomes absorbed in the spell which narrative can cast over an audience:

> He felt his audience begin to relax. The circumstances were unusual, but they were being told a story, and they were offering themselves to the story-teller in the manner of audiences down the ages, wanting to see how things turned out, wanting to have the world explained to them. (55)

With the appearance of the "visitors," Franklin, who, from behind the safety of his lectern, has spent an entire professional career carefully sequestering the ancient past from the intrusions of contemporary reality, will be catapulted into the terrors of modern history. As the drama aboard the *Santa Euphemia* unfolds, Franklin moves from "lecturer" on classical antiquity to "participant" in contemporary history—from an appreciator of history as finished aesthetic object (the dead past fossilized in its sculpture and architecture) to an active player in the making of history. Shortly after the terrorists take control of the ship, their leader addresses the hostages on the importance of understanding "'other civilizations. How they are great, and how . . . they fall'" (43). And later, when a frightened and bewildered Franklin Hughes tries to make some sense out of the crisis, the terrorist leader reminds him that as a historian, Franklin should know that "the world is not a cheerful place," adding, "I would have thought your investigations into the ancient civilizations would have taught you that. . . . We shall explain to the passengers what is happening. How they are mixed up in history. What that history is" (51). By showing him how inextricably past and present are linked, the highjacking of the *Santa Euphemia* deepens Franklin's awareness of the full meaning of history, as well as of his personal involvement in that history. As the narrator explains, Franklin, a man who puts great stock in appearances, had always disdained any situation which prevented him from being himself. Now, suddenly, he finds that history has backed him into a corner, forcing him to make a decision whose outcome could mean life or death for a fellow human being.

In his roles as television moderator and tour lecturer, Franklin makes use of a variety of rhetorical devices. For instance, his fondness for employing contemporary allusions, though in most cases his examples border on the facile (in one he likens Hannibal's elephants to Hitler's panzer divisions; in another Herod, owing to his patronage of the arts, to a "sort of Mussolini with good taste"), serves to enliven his presentations. And in his conversations with the terrorist leader, Franklin gains new respect for the chilling power of euphemism:

> 'The law, Mr. Hughes. People are always telling us what is the law. I am often puzzled by what they consider is lawful and what is unlawful'. . . . 'But it is a long argument, and sometimes I think argument is pointless, just as the law is pointless'. . . . 'As for the matter of Miss Maitland, let us hope that her nationality does not become, how shall I put it, relevant.'
> Franklin tried to damp down a shudder. There were times when euphemism could be much more frightening than direct threat. (47–48)

Later, when he is informed by the terrorist chief that it will become necessary to apply "pressure" in order to speed the negotiations up, Franklin replies "'Pressure?' Even Franklin, who could not have made a career in television without skill in trading euphemisms, was enraged. 'You mean killing people'" (50).

"The Visitors" abounds in irony, and the highjacking crisis will force Franklin to re-examine the role of this rhetorical device. For instance, Franklin initially gives the impression of being both confident in his knowledge of the ancient world and comfortable in his abilities as a lecturer; however, it soon becomes apparent that Franklin is occasionally prey to self-doubts, even though he has succeeded to some extent in concealing these beneath a thin veneer of complacency and self-delusion. As the narrator implies, there are times when Franklin feels threatened by certain types of tourists:

> ...What Franklin Hughes couldn't stand were bores with pet ideas they couldn't wait to try out on the guest lecturer. Excuse me, Mr. Hughes, it looks very Egyptian to me—how do we know the Egyptians didn't build it? Aren't you assuming that Homer wrote when people think he (a little laugh)—or she—did? I don't have any actual expert knowledge, yet surely it would make more sense if. . . . There was always at least one of them, playing the puzzled yet reasonable amateur; unfooled by received opinion, he—or she—knew that historians were full of bluff, and that complicated matters were best understood using zestful intuition untainted by any actual knowledge or research. 'I appreciate what you're saying, Mr. Hughes, but surely it would be more logical . . .' (39)

Later, while he and the terrorist leader are discussing the fate of Mr. Talbot, a tourist who claims to have misplaced his passport, Franklin muses: "'Mr. Talbot, yes.' A vague, elderly Englishman who tended to ask questions about religion in the Ancient World. A mild fellow with no theories of his own, thank God" (45).

Further exacerbated, it is hinted, by the low esteem in which many of his more learned academic counterparts hold him (they regard him as a "popularizer" of history), Franklin's self-doubts stem, in part, from his early experiences in television—in those years when he knew that he was nothing more than a "mouthpiece for other people's views, a young man in a corduroy suit with an affable and unthreatening way of explaining culture" (34). And although it is true that this feeling of being unoriginal later spurred him on to write and produce his own material, Franklin never really overcame the sense that he could not measure up to the abilities of his colleagues:

> Franklin would freely admit he was a showman and would stand on his head in a bucket of herrings if that would raise viewing figures a few thousand, but there was a residual feeling in him—a mixture of admiration and shame—which made him hold in special regard those communicators who were deeply unlike him: the ones who spoke quietly, in their own simple words, and whose stillness gave them authority. (55)

While Franklin nervously collects his thoughts just prior to delivering what turns out to be his final "lecture" of the cruise (it is the one he must make in order to save Tricia's life), the narrator explains: "before he got his own writing credit Franklin had become expert at presenting the ideas of others as plausibly as possible" (54). That Franklin will be called upon by the terrorists to deliver yet another "lecture" is a masterful irony, for as he struggles to explain the Arabs' version of history, which in this case amounts to justifying why the killing of innocent civilians is an act of "historical inevitability," Franklin finds himself in a familiar role—that of presenting the ideas of others as "plausibly as possible." Before actually delivering the speech which the terrorists force upon him, Franklin spends some tense moments searching desperately for ways to make the passengers believe that he is acting under duress. He hits upon the idea of speaking so enthusiastically about the Arab cause that the audience would not fail to miss the irony. But this plan is quickly aborted when Franklin recalls the words of one of his former TV producers: "Irony is something that people miss" (54).

Franklin's "insecurities" also surface from time to time in his self-conscious manipulation of the tourists' perceptions and attitudes. At times, for instance, he affects the pose of a jaded tour guide: "Franklin engagingly admitted that there were occasions when even he could tire of yet another row of Corinthian columns standing against a cloudless sky; though he did this in a way which allowed the passengers to disbelieve him" (38). What is more, as his "welcoming" speech reveals, Franklin could be very defensive about the public's image of television celebrities:

> The first leg of the trip, as they steamed down the Adriatic, went much as usual. There was the Welcome Buffet, with the crew sizing up the passengers and the passengers warily circling one another; Franklin's opening lecture, in which he flattered his audience, deprecated his television fame and annoucned that it was a refreshing change to be addressing real people instead of a glass eye and a cameraman shouting 'Hair in the gate, can we do it again, love?' [the technical reference would be lost on most of his listeners: they were allowed to be snobbish about TV, but not to assume it was idiots' business]. (36)

Franklin's relationships with women, which seem to be plagued by the same kinds of insecurities, self-doubts, and delusions that beset his professional life, reveal much about his character. Both areas of his life—the "academic" and the romantic—seem equally crippled by fears, inhibitions, and lack of passion—all rendered palatable by a skill with euphemism that matches the chief terrorist's own. For instance, when Franklin advises Tricia to consider their Aegean excursion as a "three weeks' holiday from the filthy English weather and all that backstabbing at Television Centre," the young woman

> nodded agreement. . . . A more worldy-wise girl would have readily understood Franklin to mean 'Don't expect more out of me than this.' Tricia, being placid and optimistic, glossed his little speech more mildly as 'Let's be careful of building

up false expectations'—which to do him credit was roughly what Franklin Hughes meant. (37)

We know that Franklin has been married twice, that he has a daughter whom he does not really know, and that he falls

> lightly in love several times each year, a tendency in himself which he would occasionally deplore but regularly indulge. However, he was far from heartless, and the moment he felt a girl—especially a nice girl—needing him more than he needed her a terrible flush of apprehension would break out in him. This rustling panic would usually make him suggest one of two things: either that the girl move into his flat, or that she move out of his life—neither of which he exactly wanted. (37)

Franklin is, all-in-all, a master of self-deception. A good example of this can be found early in the story, where the narrator remarks Franklin's fondness for describing himself as a writer in the hope that the description will make him feel like one. In another early scene, Franklin informs Tricia, whom he has gone to bed with only a couple of times, that in order to make this year's presentation a little different, he will have to spend a lot of time alone preparing his lectures. In fact, however, Franklin, who likes "to maintain the fiction of working on his lectures before hand," never varies his presentation from one year to the next: ". . . his opening address at ten the next morning would be exactly the same as for the previous five years. The only difference—the only thing designed to prevent Franklin from going stale—was the presence of Tricia instead of . . . of, what was that last girl's name?" (35). Ironically, this trip will prove to be quite different from his previous excursions into the past. The terrorist attack on the *Santa Euphemia* not only pulls Franklin into the world of living history but also forces him to confront his own nature. The final victory, it would seem, goes neither to the terrorists nor to those who battle terrorism nor to those who get caught in between—the final victory goes to irony: for in saving Tricia's life, Franklin loses her respect. But the conclusion also leaves open the possibility that in his secret knowledge of having done the right thing, Franklin has achieved the blessing of self-respect.

III

Just as the motif of "twos," or "couples," serves to link Chapters One and Two, so the re-appearance of woodworm and the continued references to Noah's Ark in Barnes' third tale, "The Wars of Religion," help to connect that story to "The Stowaway." Written in an inflated, almost mock-heroic style, "The Wars of Religion" takes place in sixteenth century France and speaks to the religious extremism and superstitions of the period, revealing the kind of fanatical excesses which promote intolerance and pave the way for such events as inquisitions and religious wars. On another level, the story looks at the ways in which truth, evidence, and testimony can be twisted to support opposing viewpoints.

But despite these rather grim undertones, "The Wars of Religion" also sparkles with humor, much of which is derived from the disproportion between the breadth of legal erudition displayed by the opposing attorneys and the actual nature and circumstances of the case being ajudicated. Barnes' motive here may be to satirize the kinds of trivial issues which have engulfed the church in conflict down through the ages. This comic/satiric effect is heightened, as was hinted above, by the "mock-heroic" quality of the story's language, particularly as it is embodied in the prosecuting attorney's bombastic rhetoric and his numerous allusions to the Bible and classical mythology:

> Gentlemen, it does me honour to appear again before your solemn court, to plead for justice as did that poor offended mother who appeared before Solomon to claim her child. Like Ulysses against Ajax I shall fight the procurator for the bestioles, who has produced before you many arguments as bedizened as Jezebel. (69)

The defendants in the case—the woodworm—are on trial for infesting the Saint-Michel church and causing so much damage to the diocesan bishop's throne that when the bishop sits on it, which he does every year as part of his annual ceremonial visit to the church, it collapses and sends him crashing to the floor, resulting in serious injury to his head.

The prosecuting attorney's opening argument centers on the woodworm's defiance in failing to appear before the court after having been served a writ of summons. He calls not only for the insects' banishment from the village but also for their excommunication from the church, arguing that since there is no record of their having been aboard Noah's Ark (and thus part of God's original creation), they must have been spawned from Satan and can, therefore, be punished without offending God in any way.

The defense attorney, a clever polemicist in his own right, is the one person who seems to appreciate the absurdity of the situation. His basic strategy is to demonstrate how the court has no jurisdiction over the insects. On the matter of excommunication, for instance, the defense argues that such an idea is unthinkable inasmuch as the woodworm do not have immortal souls and do not belong to any church from which they could be ex-communicated. He also maintains that the court has no authority to sit in judgment of God's creatures; and when his opponent argues that in *Genesis* God gave man dominion over all other living things on the earth, a position implying the power to punish "malfeasant" animals, the defense argues that man often abuses this position either through ego or ignorance.

The defense's invocation of various legal technicalities further undermines his adversary's strategies. Much of his defense is predicated on the fact that the summoning of the woodworm to court presupposes their ability to speak, read, and make rational judgments. Since, as he goes on to argue, the insects' inability to do any of these things prevents them from complying with the summons, and since the law expressly prohibits trying a defendant *in absentia*, the case must be dismissed. Furthermore, when the prosecutor attempts to persuade the court that the insects should be punished because they were not on board the Ark, the defense attorney replies that since no actual record exists indicating whether the woodworm were or were not aboard Noah's vessel, then by law it must be presumed that they were present on the ship. The defense further contends that in eating wood, the woodworm were merely following their own instincts, not engaging in criminal acts. When the prosecution rejoins that the woodworms' diet of wood, even though sanctioned by none other than God Himself, does not apply to "cut" wood, the defense attorney points out that the insects were already in the wood when it was cut, and that consequently, if any blame is to be placed, it must be placed on the woodcutters, not on the insects.

The defense demands that other aspects of the case be clarified as well. Exactly how many woodworm are to be tried? All of them? Or just those directly responsible for the bishop's injury and the weakened condition of the church's roof? And why does the court insist on targeting this particular generation of woodworm when it is certainly the case (here he cites the testimony of an authority on insect behavior) that the infestation of the church was begun years earlier by the present generation's ancestors? Furthermore, is it not possible that the visitation of the woodworm upon the church is a judgment against the parishioners for failure to tithe?

In his summation, the defense attorney continues to batten on the theme of tithes, and, not to be outdone by his opponent, he displays his own skill with allusions. Arguing that Almighty God would never stand back and permit the destruction of His church, as well as the injury of one of His ministers, if it were not for a specific purpose, he observes:

> Did [the Lord] not send a plague of frogs against Pharaoh? Did He not send lice and grievous swarms of flies upon the land of Egypt? Did He not, against the Pharaoh, send also a plague of boils, and thunder and hail, and a grievous plague of locusts? Did He not send hailstones against the Five Kings? Did He not strike even His own servant Job with boils? (76)

After advising the communicants to "cast out the beam from your own eye before you seek to extract the mote from the eye of another," the defense proposes that they resolve the crisis by setting aside a portion of land outside the village to be used as a habitation for the woodworm, and it is this proposal, together with a few additional conditions of his own, which the judge endorses in his final disposition of the case.

"The Wars of Religion" asks a lot of its readers in the way of suspending disbelief (although history does record several instances in which cats and pigs and other animals were tried for such things as witchcraft and demonic possession, no records exist of a court case involving insects), and yet Barnes takes great pains to authenticate the actual occurrence of the trial, even going so far as to provide not only specific dates and the name of a putative historical figure (the defense attorney, Monsieur Chausenee) but also prefatory background information on the archival/editorial history of the documents in which the case is recorded (including the numbers of the boxes which the documents are stored in). What is more, the narrative itself has no conclusion. Instead, the chapter ends with an editorial note which not only informs the reader of the incomplete state of the transcript but also describes its physical condition:

> Here the manuscript in the Archives Municipales de Besancon breaks off, without giving details of the annual penance imposed by the court. It appears from the condition of the parchment that in the course of the last four and a half centuries it has been attacked, perhaps on more than one occasion, by some species of termite, which has devoured the closing words of the *juge d'Eglise*. (80)

To some extent, even the prosecutor's (and on at least one occasion the defense attorney's) allusions to "actual" biblical and literary figures contributes to this effect. Thus, by creating the illusion of historical actuality, this strategy of freighting his story with documentary material—a ploy which harks back to the central fictional techniques of Daniel DeFoe—enables Barnes to further explore the relationship between literature and reality.

IV

Like James Joyce's *Dubliners*, Barnes' *A History of the World in 10 1/2 Chapters* makes use of a variety of styles and narrative forms. "The

Stowaway," for example, utilizes a fairly traditional first-person narrative voice, notwithstanding the fact that it is supplied by one of the many insects which have managed to sneak aboard Noah's Ark. "The Visitors" features a limited third-person narrator who reports events chiefly through the mind of the story's central character, Franklin Hughes. And in "The Wars of Religion," Barnes makes use of a kind of Popean mock-heroic style.

This diversity of narrative forms and styles is continued in Barnes' next story, "The Survivor," whose plot unfolds inside the dreaming mind of the main character. The story deals with a young woman named Kathleen Ferris. One day Kathleen, who has been living in Australia with a man named Greg, "steals" her boyfriend's boat and, accompanied only by two cats, Paul and Linda, sets out to sea in order to escape a nuclear war occurring somewhere in the Northern Hemisphere (Kathleen had originally lived in an undisclosed country in the "north" but, because of an impending military crisis there, had emigrated to Australia). After spending what appears to be several days at sea, Kathleen beaches-up on a deserted island, where, shortly after landing, she apparently falls asleep and re-lives her voyage in a dream. But the dream also includes other details from Kathleen's life, such as a brief episode from her days in elementary school, her belief that reindeer can fly, her fears about nuclear war and the contamination of the earth's environment, her relationship with Greg, and finally an incident which is repeatedly described as a "nightmare" or "bad dream"—her supposed incarceration in a psychiatric hospital.

One obstacle in reading "The Survivor" is the difficulty in determining which of the events recounted in Kathleen's dream actually happened to her and which are merely "fictions" within that dream. In the part of the story which deals with her hospitalization, for example, the doctors inform Kathleen that she never reached an island, as she believed she had, but rather was rescued "About a hundred miles east of Darwin. Going round in circles" (109). The doctors attribute Kathleen's illness to "persistent victim syndrome," or "PVS" (an ironic twist on the pre-menstrual tension, or PMT, which Greg attributes it to)—meaning, presumably, that she is victimized by the enormous emotional investment she makes in her relationships with men. Frightened by her possessiveness, the men first abuse and then leave her. When Kathleen attempts to convince the doctors that they are mistaken—that it was not trouble with Greg which induced her to undertake her voyage, but fear of nuclear war—the doctors propose that she is fabulating: "You make up a story to cover the facts you don't know or can't accept. You keep a few true facts and spin a new story round them" (109) (the introduction of this term raises the story to a metafictional level insofar as "fabulation" becomes a metaphor for exactly what Barnes himself is doing in the book: keeping a few true facts and spinning a new story around them). In this section of the story, Kathleen seems to be aware that she is dreaming, that she is wrestling with her own mind. And at the very end of the chapter, we read that "The next day, on a small, scrubby island in the Torres Straits, Kath Ferris woke up to find that Linda had given birth" (111)—a detail which seems to suggest that Kathleen's "hospital" dream is fictional, a dream within a dream.

To complicate matters even further, Kathleen's dream is rendered in alternating first and third person narrative voices. Barnes' use of oscillating narratives is somewhat reminiscent of the strategy Dickens employs in *Bleak House*. In Dickens' case, however, the alternating narrators provide complementary visions of the novel's social world—one a private mode of vision, the other a public. As Jacob Korg observes:

> The profound and subtle oscillations introduced by the alternating narrative voices prevents *Bleak House* from formulating its moral problems in fixed images. They appear in ambiguous form, as matters of social responsibility when seen through the eyes of the objective narrator, and as matters of private conscience when seen through Esther's. (20)

In "The Survivor," by contrast, Barnes' use of alternating first and third person points-of-view enables him not only to achieve an extraordinary juxtaposition of dream and reality but also to expose the different "ontological" levels of fictional elements (the Chinese-box structuring of a dream within a dream within a fiction).

But this alternation of narrative voices also places additional burdens on the reader, for although both points-of-view provide different angles of vision, they frequently converge on the same action, making it difficult to unravel the two main narrative strands (Kathleen's narrative and the third-person narrative). The "omniscient" narrator, who seems at times to function as a "chorus," is a kind of Jamesian voice that reports events through a central consciousness (in this case the consciousness of the main character). The third-person provides the outer scaffolding of the story, chiefly by "externalizing" the main character's perceptions and mental states, while the first-person narrator transmits Kathleen's thoughts, as well as other intimate details of her life, directly. For example, on at least three occasions the third-person narrator merely informs us that Kathleen is having bad dreams. The first-person narrator then presents the actual contents of the dreams.

Like other stories in *A History of the World in 10 1/2 Chapters*, "The Survivor" recalls several of the motifs first encountered in "The

Stowaway." For instance, each story evokes a world on the brink of cataclysmic disaster, for just as in chapter one the earth is wiped out by God's Flood, so in "The Survivor" human life is endangered by the imminent threat of nuclear war. Moreover, Kathleen Ferris, the story's eponymous "survivor," grieves for the fate of the reindeer, whose premonitions of disaster were voiced by the narrator of "The Stowaway." Kathleen's reflections on "The Survival of the Worriers," in which she wonders whether the reindeer had ever been troubled by fears of approaching danger, recall the reindeers' state of agitated pre-science aboard Noah's Ark in chapter one:

> Only those who can see what's happening will survive, that must be the rule. I bet there were animals who sensed the Ice Age was coming and set off on some long and dangerous journey to find a safer, warmer climate. . . . I wonder if the reindeer saw what was going to happen to them. Do you think they even sensed it somehow? (97)

Another link between "The Survivor" and the first story (as well as "The Visitors") is supplied by the recurrence of the "twos" or "pairs" theme. As a child, Kathleen envisioned the reindeer "harnessed side by side" pulling Santa's sleigh on Christmas Eve. She "always imagined that each pair was man and wife, a happy couple, like the animals that went into the Ark" (90). When Kathleen flees Australia in her boyfriend's boat, she brings "two" cats with her. And later, when Kathleen thinks about the island on which she imagines her journey will end, we find this passage:

> She didn't think she was going to land on some undamaged island where you only had to throw a bean over your shoulder for a row of them to spring up and wave their pods at you. She didn't expect a coral reef, a strip of sand from the holiday brochures and a nodding palm. She didn't imagine some good-looking fellow turning up after a couple weeks in a dinghy with two dogs on board; then a girl with two chickens, a bloke with two pigs, and so on. (92)

As Kathleen continues sailing, she imagines the sea filled with people just like herself, all navigating little "arks" of their own:

> I'm sure I'm not alone. I mean, I'm sure everywhere in the world there are people like me. It can't be just me, just me alone in a boat with two cats. I bet there are hundreds, thousands of boats with people in and animals doing what I'm doing. (94)

At the end of her odyssey, Kathleen's female cat, Linda, gives birth to kittens, an event which recalls the regeneration of life after the voyage of Noah's Ark.

"The Survivor" also touches on important ecological issues. In one section of the story the narrator alludes to the Chernobyl nuclear disaster. Kathleen feels that the radioactive poisons released by Chernobyl are blowing all over the planet. She complains of skin irritations and later is told that her hair is falling out—two typical symptoms of exposure to radioactive fallout. In another part of the story, Barnes evokes a landscape of rusting machinery:

> The rocks over here were strewn with discarded bits of metal—engines, boilers, valves, pipes, all turning orangey-brown with rust. As she walked, she stirred up flocks of orangey-brown butterflies which had started to live among the scrap metal, using it as camouflage. What have we done to the butterflies, she thought; look where we've made them live. (91)

In addition, Kathleen expresses her fear for the welfare of animals, particularly the reindeer, which, as we have already seen, have become irradiated by fallout from Chernobyl. She also worries about the pollution of the oceans and laments the fact that at the dock where Greg's boat is moored, people have to pay to feed the fish: "We live," she observes, "in a world where they make children pay to see the fish eat. Nowadays even fish are exploited. Exploited and then poisoned. The ocean out there is filling up with poison. The fish will die too" (91). Finally, in a passage which recalls the brutal mistreatment of animals aboard Noah's Ark in "The Stowaway," the third-person narrator asks, "Why are we always punishing the animals? We pretend we like them, we keep them as pets and get soppy if we think they're reacting like us, but we've been punishing animals from the beginning, haven't we? Killing them and torturing them and throwing our guilt on to them?" (92).

Foucaultian themes reverberate throughout the story as well. On one level each of the stories discussed so far allegorizes the conflict between those who control the machinery of repressive power and those who are the victims of that power—the masses of the dispossessed and the defenseless. In "The Stowaway" God's power over Noah (we might recall that God is referred to in that story as Noah's "oppressive role-model") is mirrored by the almost unrestricted power that Noah and his family wield against the animals. In "The Visitors" power struggles exist on several levels: there is Franklin's "power" as lecturer over the tourists; the West's (including Israel's) power over the Third World Arab states; and the terrorists' power over the hostages (and by extension, over the Western world). And in "The Wars of Religion" the ecclesiastical court exercises its power over the woodworm. Similarly, in "The Survivor" we witness a world brutalized by immense corporate, military, and political power structures—this time through the eyes of a young woman. For Kathleen, who always sees "connections" in things, "men in dark-grey suits with striped ties" become a kind of synecdoche for the oligarchic power-cliques which control the world. When Kathleen's boy-friend Greg informs her that he intends on spending his evenings patronizing the local taverns instead of coming home to her, she attributes his inconstancy to global politics:

> [Greg] said he was staying out because he couldn't stand coming home and getting nagged at by me, I told him I undertsood and it was all right, yet when I explained he got very uptight. He said if he wanted a bit on the side then it wouldn't be because of the world situation but because I was on his back all the time. They just don't see the connections, do they? When men in dark-grey suits and striped ties up there in the north start taking certain strategic precautions as they term it, men like Greg in tongs and T-shirts down here in the south begin staying out late in bars trying to pick up girls. (89–90)

As the preceding passage suggests, these power struggles also manifest themselves in gender conflicts—a theme which had been prefigured early in the story when, as a child, Kathleen learns the true sexual identity of Santa's reindeer:

> . . . her Dad said you could tell from the antlers that the reindeer pulling the sleigh were stags. At first she only felt disappointment, but later resentment grew. Father Christmas ran an all-male team. Typical. Absolutely bloody typical, she thought. (83)

As a young woman, Kathleen finds herself victimized by her boyfriend's sexist attitudes. An inveterate beer drinker with a fondness for both seducing and slapping women, Greg represents power in its crudest and most vulgar form. He often dismisses Kathleen's fears and concerns about the world political situation as mere symptoms of pre-menstrual tension, arguing that "politics is men's business." When Kathleen tries to convince her boyfriend that his remarks about pre-menstrual tension are truer than he thinks because "women are more closely connected to all the cycles of nature and birth and rebirth on the planet than men, who are only impregnators after all" (89), Greg merely repeats, "Silly cow, that's just why politics is men's business." A few days later, when Kathleen and Greg continue their argument about the "Big Thing," Greg's comments reveal what many recent feminist theorists have identified as Western culture's domination by "phallocentric" powers:

> [Greg] said to me, what happened about the end of the world? I just looked at him and he said, as far as I can see all that premenstrual tension you had was about the fact that you were getting your period. I said you make me so angry I almost want the end of the world to come just so you'll be proved wrong. He said he was sorry, but what did he know, after all he was just an impregnator as I'd pointed out, and he reckoned those other impregnators up in the north would sort something out. (89)

Moreover, while in the hospital, Kathleen notes that the doctors are "always men," and she often refers to them as "tempters"—a contemporary twist, perhaps, on the old idea of women as "temptresses."

This identification of power with maleness surfaces again in Kathleen's tirade against "famous men":

> There was a battle here, a war there, a king was deposed, famous men—always famous men, I'm sick of famous men—made events happen. . . . All I see is the old connections, the ones we don't take any notice of any more because that makes it easier to poison reindeer and feed them to mink. Who made that happen? Which famous man will claim credit for that? (97)

Kathleen's sea voyage is a flight from all the cumulative terrors of a male-centered world. She repudiates the idea of history as a chronicle of events enacted by "famous men"; nor does she place much value in dates: "Names, dates, achievements. I hate dates. Dates are bullies, dates are know-alls" (99). These aversions to dates and famous men are closely intertwined with Kathleen's inability to remember the rest of the rhyme about Columbus that "Western" school children are required to learn: "In fourteen hundred and ninety-two/Columbus sailed the ocean blue" (opening the way, incidentally, for European exploitation of the new world). Ironically, Kathleen associates the Columbus jingle with an act of schoolroom "violence" perpetrated against her by one of her male classmates:

> In fourteen hundred and ninety-two
> Columbus sailed the ocean blue.
>
> And then what? She couldn't remember. All those years ago obedient ten-year-olds with arms crossed, they had chanted it back to the mistress. All except Eric Dooley, who sat behind her and chewed her pigtail. Once she'd been asked to get up and recite the next two lines but she was only a few inches out of her seat when her head snapped back and the class laughed. Eric was hanging on to her plait with his teeth. Perhaps that was why she could never remember the next two lines. (83)

For Kathleen, "history" is not a cavalcade of dates, events, and famous men, but rather a return to more ancient, more primitive ways of doing things. Insisting that the future lies in the past, Kathleen looks forward to the time when man will no longer "measure things in days any more. Days and weekends and holidays—that's how the men in grey suits measure things. We'll have to go back to some older cycle, sunrise to sunset for a start, and the moon will come into it, and the seasons, and the weather" (93). While on the boat, she refuses to divide the food rations between herself and the cats on the basis of how long she might be at sea because "That's the old sort of thinking, the thinking that led us into all this" (93). Looking back on her sexual relations with Greg, Kathleen comes to the conclusion that "All that side of things seems odd now. Bits of rubber and tubes to squeeze and pills to swallow. There won't be any of that any more. We're going to give ourselves back to nature now" (97).

Man must return to a more natural way of life because he is headed on a course of self-destruction. Swiftian tones can be detected in Barnes' satirical indictment of modern technology, especially modern military technology. Man's ingenuity in refining the instruments of destruction (we may recall Gulliver's pride in Europe's state-of-the-art munitions) will, if left unchecked, lead to the extinction of the human race. This point is nicely driven home when Kathleen decides that it was the mind "that was the cause of it all. The mind simply got too clever for its own good, it got carried away. It was the mind that invented these weapons, wasn't it? You couldn't imagine an animal inventing its own destruction, could you?" (102). She then tells herself a story about a bear which gets killed in its own trap. One day, after digging a deep pit, placing a sharp stake in the bottom of it, and camouflaging the whole thing with branches and undergrowth, the bear lumbers home:

> Now where do you think the bear had dug its pit? Right in the middle of one of its own favorite trails, a spot it regularly crossed on its way to drink honey from the trees, or whatever it is bears do. So the next day the bear lolloped along the path, fell into the pit and got impaled on the stake. As it died it thought. My, my, this is a surprise, what a curious way things have turned out. Perhaps it was a mistake to dig a trap where I did. Perhaps it was a mistake do dig a trap in the first place.
>
> You can't imagine a bear doing that, can you? But that's what it's like with us, she reflected. (103)

The parable affords us a chilling vision of a world bent on its own destruction. Within this whirlwind of mass insanity, Kathleen's tiny voice affirms life and the value of all living creatures.

V

In his fifth chapter, "Shipwreck," Barnes once again explores the relation of history to art. In it the author focuses special attention on the ways in which both natural and human catastrophes, like the Chernobyl nuclear disaster of the preceding story, are transmuted into painting and other aesthetic forms. At the beginning of the second part of the chapter Barnes ponders this problem:

> How do we turn catastrophe into art?
> Nowadays the process is automatic. A nuclear plant explodes? We'll have a play on the London stage within a year. A President is assassinated? You can have the book or the film or the filmed book or the booked film. War? Send in the novelists. A series of gruesome murders? Listen for the tramp of the poets. We have to understand it, of course, this catastrophe; to understand it we have to imagine it, so we need the imaginative arts. But we also need to justify it and forgive it, this catastrophe, however minimally. Why did it happen, this mad act of Nature, this crazed human moment? Well, at least it produced art. Perhaps, in the end, that's what catastrophe is for. (125)

In this story, which contains an exposition of Gericault's painting "Scene of Shipwreck," Barnes continues his use of connective images and motifs. For instance, the perilous voyage of the *Medusa*'s raft recalls Kathleen Ferris' odyssey on the Pacific Ocean in "The Survivor." Moreover, echoes of "The Stowaway" can be found in the section of "Shipwreck" where Barnes provides a brief account of the history of paintings of Noah's Ark. In addition, Barnes informs us that in order "To make the shadow as black as possible, Gericault used quantities of bitumen"—the same substance that Noah used in the construction of his ark. Finally, Barnes notes that "Our leading expert on Gericault confirms that ['Scene of Shipwreck'] is 'now in part a ruin.' And no doubt if they examine the frame they will discover woodworm living there" (139).

"Shipwreck" is divided into two parts. Part I is a documentary narrative which deals with the ill-fated voyage of the *Medusa*. The presumed source of Barnes' information for this first part of the chapter is a book co-authored by Messieurs Savigny and Correard, two survivors of the *Medusa* disaster. The *Medusa*, a French frigate, was part of an expeditionary flotilla to Senegal. Embarking from France in June 1816, the flotilla proceeded apace until a combination of heavy winds and poor navigation dispersed the ships. After several days of sailing alone, the *Medusa* struck a reef off the coast of Africa, sustaining sufficient damage to warrant an evacuation. A large raft was constructed to accommodate the crewmembers and passengers who could not fit on the ship's regular life-boats. According to the original evacuation plan, the raft was to be loaded with some food supplies (mainly casks of wine and water, and flour for biscuits) and 150 people. Once loaded, the raft was to be towed to shore by the *Medusa*'s four life boats. As Barnes points out, however, though the "plan was perfectly well-laid, it was traced upon loose sand, which was dispersed by the breath of egotism" (116).

Straightaway things went wrong. As soon as the "abandon-ship" order came, panic began to grip the crewmembers who had not been assigned places on the lifeboats. The loading and embarkation of the raft became completely disorganized. What is more, the tiny vessel immediately began to submerge under the weight of its cargo of people and provisions. To lessen the burden many of the wine and water casks were thrown overboard. When order was finally restored, the tow-lines were fastened and the life-boats began pulling the raft. But without warning, the lines were suddenly disconnected: "One by one, whether for reasons of self-interest, incompetence, misfortune or seeming necessity, the tow-ropes were cast aside" (117). The raft began to drift out to sea. Having neither oars to row with, rudder to steer with, or compass to navigate with, the raft and its crewmembers were completely at the mercy of the elements. There ensued several unimaginably terrible days at sea.

The hopes of the castaways rose and fell like the very waves which lashed their tiny "ark." One day a white butterfly appeared. The unexpected sight of this delicate insect so near the raft inspired conflicting emotions among the men. To those "crazed with hunger, it seemed that even this could make a morsel. To others, the ease with which their visitor moved appeared a very mockery when they lay exhausted and almost motionless beneath it. To yet others, this simple butterfly was a sign, a messenger from Heaven as white as Noah's dove" (121). But whereas for Noah the dove's olive branch meant that the flood waters had subsided, for the men aboard the raft, the signs of land would continue to elude them.

Owing to storms, starvation, mutinies, delirium, and suicides, the raft's original complement of 150 crewmembers was soon reduced to 28. Of this number, 13 were too weak to survive the next twenty-four hours, whereupon it was decided by the fifteen stronger castaways that they should be thrown into the sea in order to conserve food. This action, in which "The healthy were separated from the unhealthy like the clean from the unclean" (121), recalls the culling of animals in "The Stowaway" and hostages in "The Visitors."

As the situation aboard the raft continued to worsen, desperate measures were taken to combat hunger and thirst. By the fifth day, for instance, all had "learned to consume human flesh." Later, thirst became so unbearable that the "men began to moisten their lips with their own urine. They drank it from little tin cups which they first placed in water to cool their inner liquid the quicker" (121).

On their thirteenth day at sea, one of the men spotted a ship on the horizon. He alerted his comrades, but their desperate attempt to hail the ship proved futile, and "From joy they fell into despondency and grief; they envied the fate of those who had died before them." This image of the survivors waving furiously to attract the attention of the *Argus* (as well, perhaps, as the very use of the word "survivors" to describe their plight) recalls the section in the preceding story where Kathleen Ferris reflects on the perils of modern seamanship:

> There was one thing she couldn't ever forget from the article. It said that in the old days there was always someone up in the Crow's nest or on the bridges, watching for trouble. But nowadays the big ships didn't have a lookout any more, or at least the lookout was just a man staring from time to time at a screen with a lot of blips on it. In the old days if you were lost at sea in a raft or a dinghy or something, and a boat came along, there was a pretty good chance of being rescued. You waved and shouted and fired off any rockets you had; you ran your shirt to the top of the mast; and there were always people keeping an eye out for you. Nowadays you can drift on the ocean for weeks, and a supertanker finally comes along, and it goes right past. The radar won't pick you up because you're too small, and it's pure luck if anybody happens to be hanging over the rail being sick. There had been lots of cases where castaways who would have been rescued in the old days simply weren't picked up; and even incidents of people being run down by ships they thought were coming to rescue them. . . . That's what's wrong with the world, she thought. We've given up having lookouts. We don't think about saving other people, we just sail on by relying on our machines. Everyone's below deck, having a beer with Greg. (95–96)

When the raft was finally spotted by the *Argus* several hours later, only fifteen men remained alive.

For Savigny and Correard, the two men who wrote about the incident, the *Medusa* affair reflected the corruption, incompetence, and arrogance of not only the French naval officer-class but also the government which had appointed them. Incited by the writings of Savigny and Correard, disaffected intellectuals and political malcontents all over France elevated the *Medusa* scandal to a *cause celebre*.

Having recounted a historical event (the *Medusa* "catastrophe") in the first part of "Shipwreck," Barnes next turns his attention to the world of art. In Part II of his narrative, which is an essay on both the genesis and technical execution of Gericault's painting "Scene of Shipwreck," Barnes attempts to answer the question he had posed at the beginning of the chapter: "How do you turn catastrophe into art?"

You do so, the essay seems to imply, by departing from the actual facts. Gericault began his work by familiarizing himself with all the documentary details of the case. After reading Savigny and Correard's book, he interviewed the two writers at some length. He even persuaded the former castaways to serve as models for the painting (and thus in effect "relive" their terrifying experience aboard the raft—a detail which will link "Shipwreck" with a later story). Next, Gericault commissioned the *Medusa*'s carpenter (who had survived the ordeal) to construct a scale replica of the raft, onto which he placed small wax figures to represent the castaways in various positions. In addition, the artist surrounded himself with "his own paintings of severed heads and dissected limbs, to infiltrate the air with mortality."

Despite Gericault's meticulous accumulation of factual data, however, "Scene of Shipwreck" is not a "truthful" representation of the *Medusa* incident. Somewhere along "the invisible thread between eye and brush-tip" art and reality part company. In a statement which seems to embody the chapter's main theme, Barnes says, "Truth to life, at the start, to be sure; yet once the process gets under way, truth to art is the greater allegiance" (135). But precisely where does Gericault's canvas diverge from the facts? The three most crucial differences between the painting and the written record of the tragedy supplied by Savigny and Correard are the number and condition of the men aboard the raft and the rescue scene. According to the two writers, there were fifteen men on the raft when it was picked up by the *Argus*, but the painting shows twenty (five of whom—apparently from the group of thirteen who were thrown overboard—have been dragged "back from the deep to help out with [Gericault's] composition"). Moreover, Barnes remarks how "well-muscled" and healthy-looking the men are (including the dead men)—a detail which not only both departs from Savigny and Correard's description and defies reason (considering the ordeal the men had been through) but also underscores the conflict between art and life:

> We admire the way Gericault sought out the *Medusa*'s carpenter and had him build a scale model of the raft . . . but . . . but if he bothered to get the raft right, why couldn't he do the same thing with its inhabitants? . . . . These are men

who have drunk their own urine, gnawed leather from their hats, consumed their own comrades. Five of the fifteen did not survive their rescue very long. So why do they look as if they have just come from a body-building class? (135–136)

Savigny and Correard report that the *Argus* was initially sighted while still a great distance away from the raft. To hail it, one of the castaways made a flag by attaching a large white sheet to barrel hoops which he had straightened out. He then stood on one of the remaining casks and waved to the distant ship. When this attempt to call attention to himself and his comrades failed, the men crawled under a lean-to they had fashioned from one of the raft's sails and spent what they presumed would be their last hours of life in deep despair. About three hours later, however, one of the men emerged from the tent and spotted the *Argus* bearing down on the raft. The ship's captain then dispatched his life-boats to pick up the castaways.

In the painting, by contrast, three or four castaways can be seen hailing the ship, which appears as a tiny speck on the distant horizon (Barnes' explanation for the change from one to four spotters reveals the painter's concern for the formal aspects of his art: "reality offered [Gericault] a monkey-up-a-stick image; art suggested a solider focus and an extra vertical"). The scene offers no visual clues to indicate whether the ship is moving toward the raft or away from it (Barnes maintains that this is precisely Gericault's purpose—to keep the viewer suspended between hope and despair). The emotional extremes—the highs and lows of elation and despondency—associated with the respective opposing directions of the ship are embodied in the painting's formal composition. The dramatic muscular contours of the castaways' bodies lead the eye inexorably up to the highest figures in the painting—the cluster of men hailing the far-off ship. The viewer remarks the furious energy of their waving (heightened by the possibility that it may prove futile). The hailers are looking into what appears to be the first light of day—a traditional symbol of hope and new beginnings. The heavy dark clouds above and to the sides of the raft seem to be dispersing, giving way to the yellow tints of the morning sky (which could, as Barnes hastens to point out, just as easily be the yellow tints of an early evening sky). Because of the kinds of emotional responses that details such as these elicit in the viewer, he or she may conclude that the ship is moving toward the raft and that the men will soon be rescued.

However, this grouping is formally counterbalanced by the bearded figure who sits on the opposite side of the canvas gazing out at the viewer—a look of blank resignation etched into his face as the body of a dead shipmate lies draped across his lap. For Barnes, because the "greybeard's" presence elicits emotions which are the opposite of hope, he "becomes as powerful a force in the painting as that of the hailer" (132). The writer goes on by arguing that

> this counterbalance suggests the following deduction: that the picture represents the mid-point of that first sighting of the *Argus*. The vessel has been in view for a quarter of an hour and has another fifteen minutes to offer. Some believe it is still coming towards them; some are uncertain and waiting to see what happens; some—including the wisest head on board—know that it is headed away from them, and that they will not be saved. This figure incites us to read 'Scene of Shipwreck' as an image of hope being mocked. (132)

Positioned in the middle section of the canvas—between the hailers and the bearded man—we find not only dead figures but also men who are obviously delirious, uncertain, and frightened. Appropriately, they inhabit the darkest area of the painting. These figures, together with the bearded man, help make the viewer's response to the painting more equivocal. As Barnes puts it: "do we vote for the optimistic yellowing sky, or for the grieving greybeard? Or do we end up believing both versions? The eye can flick from one mood, and one interpretation, to the other: is this what was intended?" (133).

Gericault eschews "Shrivelled flesh, suppurating wounds, Belsen cheeks" because such details, though capable of eliciting "pity" and "indignation," would nevertheless act "on us too directly" (136). Barnes' analysis of the painting suggests that Gericault created a canvas which evokes a more ambiguous emotional response. A scene depicting beleaguered castaways in "tattered rags" would have been, according to Barnes, in "the same emotional register as that butterfly, the first impelling us to an easy desolation as the second impels us to an easy consolation" (136). "Scene of Shipwreck," Barnes continues,

> . . . is full of muscle and dynamism. The figures on the raft are like the waves: beneath them, yet also through them, surges the energy of the ocean. Were they painted in life-like exhaustion they would be mere dribbles of spume rather than formal conduits. It is because the figures are sturdy enough to transmit such power that the canvas unlooses in us deeper, submarinous emotions, can shift us through currents of hope and despair, elation, panic and resignation. (137)

For Barnes, "the painting has slipped history's anchor. This is no longer 'Scene of Shipwreck,' let alone 'The Raft of the *Medusa*'" (137). The artist's vision and painstaking selection of details transforms an historical event into an image of the human condition, a visual allegory of man's unceasing pursuit of dreams and ambitions which may in the end prove unobtainable.

VI

"The Mountain" and "Project Ararat," two stories which recount expeditions to "Noah's" mountain made some 130 years apart, evince such striking parallels that they can be read as companion pieces. Perhaps the most obvious thematic link between the two stories is that they both deal with one of Western history's most divisive intellectual crises—the conflict between science and religion.

"The Mountain" begins in Dublin in the late 1830s and relates the story of Amanda Fergusson, a dour, spinsterly, and—where religion is concerned—somewhat inflexible woman, whose ostensible purpose in journeying to Mt. Ararat is to rescue the soul of her recently deceased father from what she is convinced will be certain damnation owing to the old gentleman's heretical views on the church. Accompanying Amanda on her "pilgrimage" to Ararat is Miss Logan, a long-time friend of the Fergusson family.

The two women's first task is to collect all the equipment that they will need for their trip (a task which will be duplicated by the two men who make the same journey in "Project Ararat"). Along with the many items they pack, the two women also take two water-bottles, which they intend to fill with the juice from Noah's vineyards. In addition to these items, "Miss Logan understood gunpowder to be the most acceptable offering for the Turkish peasant, and writing paper for the superior classes. A common box-compass, she had been further advised, would afford pleasure by directing the Mussulman to the point of his prayers" (150) (the two "pilgrims" in "Project Ararat" offer gifts of Jimmy Carter campaign buttons to their Turkish hosts). Although she agrees to take along the gunpowder and stationery, Amanda, who was "disinclined to assist the heathen in his false adorations" (150), balks at the compass—a gesture which reveals her religious intolerance.

With the preparations at a close, the two women begin their journey. Along the way they experience many things which both shock and beguile them. As they near their destination, Amanda becomes increasingly appalled by the practices of the Eastern clergy and their followers, while Miss Logan, whose knowledge of European culture does not extend beyond the eastern boundaries of Italy, remains in a perpetual state of bewilderment. In one village the women notice a young devotee placing a small object inside a crevice in a wall near the main door of a church. On closer inspection, the object turns out to be a human tooth. Moments later, when Amanda discovers that the crevice is "stuffed full with yellowing incisors and weathered molars," she launches a tirade against the superstitions of the Eastern Church.

Far from assuaging the agitations of her soul, the journey continues to fuel Amanda's outrage over the "laxity" of Eastern Christendom. While in Russia, for instance, she argues with an Armenian priest about the advisability of scaling Mt. Ararat. The priest maintains that the climb had never been attempted—that, indeed, it had been forbidden—and he admonishes the women to go no farther. According to the holy man:

> The mountain before them was the birthplace of mankind; and he referred the ladies, while excusing himself with an ingratiating laugh for mentioning an indelicate subject, to the authority of Our Saviour's words to Nicodemus, where it is stated that a man cannot enter a second time into his mother's womb and be born once more. (155)

To make matters worse, the priest, before taking leave of his guests, tries to sell them a piece of bitumen which he claims had come from the hull of Noah's Ark. When Amanda asks how such an object could have come into his possession if no one had ever ascended the mountain, the priest replies, "Perhaps a bird had carried it down, as the dove had borne the olive branch. Or it might have been brought by an angel" (155). Meanwhile, in a passage which recalls the previous chapter's essay on Gericault's painting, Miss Logan, who was "embarrassed by Our Lord's words to Nicodemus," steers her attention in the direction of the bitumen: "was that not," she asks herself, "the material used by artists to blacken the shadows in their paintings?" (155). And while she is absorbed in these reflections, Amanda

> had merely been put into a temper: first by the attempt to thrust some foolish meaning on to the scriptural verse; and second by the priest's brazen commercial behaviour. She had yet to be impressed by the Eastern clergy, who not only countenanced belief in the miraculous powers of human teeth, but actually traded in bogus religious relics. It was monstrous. They should be punished for it. No doubt they would be. (156)

—for which sentiments, Miss Logan, who about this time begins to entertain doubts about the depth of her companion's compassion, merely "examined her employer apprehensively."

The next stop on Amanda and Miss Logan's itinerary is the Monastery of St. James, located in the village of Arghuri. Before arriving there the women catch their first sight of Great Ararat and Little Ararat. The comparative differences in height and shape between the two mountains remind Amanda "of the primal divide in the human race between the two sexes" (156). However, she does not "communicate this reflection to Miss Logan, who so far proved dismally unreceptive to the transcendental" (156). At this point Miss Logan, who plays a kind of Sancho Panza to Amanda's Quixote, raises certain questions about the actual landing of the Ark: "Had the peak risen up from the waters and punctured the keel, thereby skewering the vessel in place? For if not, how otherwise had the Ark avoided a precipitous descent as the waters had receded?" (156). To this, the unflappable Miss Fergusson offers two answers, the first of which—based on Marco Polo's theory that Mt. Ararat was cube-shaped—she herself dismisses. The more likely explanation, argues Amanda, is the one provided by previous explorers of the mountain, who reported discovering a "gently sloping valley" near the summit. "As a place of disembarkation," reasons Amanda, "it would be both natural and safe" (156). This answer, which apparently does little to enlighten Miss Logan's "pedestrian turn of mind," induces the latter to ask: "So the Ark did not land on the very summit?" (156) (In "Project Ararat" we witness the same kind of verbal sparring between the leader of the expedition and his traveling companion, whose occasional displays of incredulity echo those of Miss Logan).

The monastery which Amanda and her companion visit is reported to have been built on the site where Noah first settled after disembarking. As the women enter the abbey grounds, they are introduced to a priest whose affable demeanor, while impressing Miss Logan favorably, nevertheless irritates Amanda, who misconstrues it as a kind of lubricious obsequiousness. This impression is confirmed in her mind when the priest invites the women into his room and asks them to spend the night at the monastery. The final affront to Amanda, however, occurs when the priest serves the ladies wine:

> 'Tell me, the grapes from which this wine has been made, where are they grown?'
> The Archimandrite spread both his hands and circled to indicate the neighboring countryside.
> 'And the vines from which the grapes were plucked, who first planted them?'
> 'Our ancestor and forefather, parent of us all, Noah.'
> Miss Fergusson summed up the exchange so far, needless as this seemed to her companion. 'You are serving us the fermented grapes from Noah's vines?'
> 'It is my honour, Madam.' He smiled again. He seemed to expect if not especial thanks, at least some expression of wonder. (159)

Instead, Amanda grabs her companion and storms out of the priest's cell: "'It is a blasphemy,' said Miss Fergusson eventually. 'A blasphemy. On Noah's mountain. He lives like a farmer. He invites women to stay with him. He ferments the grape of the Patriarch. It is a blasphemy.'" Moments later, she proclaims:

> We shall ascend the mountain. Sin must be purged with water. The sin of the world was purged by the waters of the flood. It is a double blasphemy that the monk commits. We shall fill our bottles with snow from the holy mountain. The pure juice of Noah's vine we came in search of has been rendered impure. We shall bring back purging water instead. (160)

—to which "Miss Logan nodded, in startled acquiescence rather than agreement" (160).

One or two days after their ascent, which they make with the assistance of a Kurdish guide, the women witness an earthquake that destroys the monastery far below them (in 1840 the Monastery of St. James was actually destroyed by an earthquake). Amanda, still reeling from her tussle with the monk over Noah's wine, sees the disaster as an act of divine retribution, whereas Miss Logan tries to "express the view that to her humble and ignorant mind the punishment seemed excessive" (163).

The next day, as the women and their guide continue to climb, Amanda injures herself in a fall. After cleaning her up and getting her back on her feet, Miss Logan and the Kurd carry Amanda around on their shoulders for the remainder of the day. Towards nightfall, they spot two small caves in the side of the mountain. As she is being carried into one of the caves, Amanda asks to be placed in a position which will afford her a good view of the full moon she has seen rising over the mountain range.

The following day, Miss Logan and the guide climb down the mountain to get help. Upon reaching the nearest village, however, the Kurd decamps, and Miss Logan is told by one of the village elders that because of the recent earthquake, organizing a rescue party would be next to impossible. Unable to save her friend, Miss Logan returns to Ireland shortly afterwards.

She spends much of her journey home puzzling over the circumstances surrounding her companion's "fall." The accident had occurred on a "flattish stretch of granite" which, as far as Miss Logan could ascertain, posed little threat of danger. Reflecting on the change which had come over her companion during the expedition (she "did not fully understand her employer's condition of mind. Having come this great distance to intercede for her father, she [Amanda] now seemed instead to be constantly arguing with his shade" [167]), Miss Logan wrestles with the possibility that Amanda might have intentionally thrown herself down "in order to achieve or confirm whatever it was she wanted to achieve or confirm" (168).

In the beginning of "The Mountain," Amanda's attitudes are pitted againt those of her curmudgeonly, sceptical, and practical-minded father, whose penchant for scientific, as opposed to theological, explanations of natural phenomena never fails to exasperate his "devout" daughter. As this temperamental rift between father and daughter widens, they find themselves embroiled in countless arguments. In one scene which not only links "The Mountain" to the preceding story but also reveals the immense gulf separating "genuine" art from "vulgar" art, Amanda and her father squabble over Monsieur Gericault's famous pictorial rendition of the *Medusa* disaster. After promising to take his daughter to see "Scene of Shipwreck," which is on loan to a Dublin art museum, Mr. Fergusson decides instead that he would prefer to go to the Pavilion, where he can feast his eyes on "Messrs Marshall's Marine Peristrephic Panorama of the Medusa French Frigate and the Fatal Raft." As Mr. Fergusson explains it, not only is the admission price cheaper at the Pavilion, but the theater is heated by "patent stoves." What is more, the narrator states:

> Whereas the Rotunda displayed a mere twenty-four feet by eighteen of stationary pigment, here they were offering some 10,000 square feet of mobile canvas. Before their eyes an immense picture, or series of pictures, gradually unwound: not just one scene, but the entire history of the shipwreck passed before them. Episode succeeded episode, while coloured lights played upon the unreeling fabric, and an orchestra emphasized the drama of events. . . . In the sixth scene those poor French wretches on the raft were represented in very much the same posture as that in which they had been first delineated by Monsieur Jerricualt. But how much grander, Mr. Fergusson observed, to picture their tragic plight with movement and coloured lights, accompanied by music. (145)

Undaunted by her father's belief that the "way forward" lies in such technological geegaws as "Messrs Marshall's Marine Peristrephic Panorama" and "patent stoves," Amanda returns to Dublin the following week to see the Gericault exhibit: "There she greatly admired Monsieur Jerricault's canvas, which though static contained for her much motion and lighting, and, in its own way, music—indeed in some fashion it contained more of these things than did the vulgar panorama" (145–146).

Most of their arguments, however, center on the conflict between science and religion. As the narrator observes: "Where Amanda discovered in the world divine intent, benevolent order and rigorous justice, her father had seen only chaos, hazard and malice. Yet they were examining the same world" (148). Not surprisinlgy, perhaps, Amanda's belief in God, which is predicated, in part, on a kind of watered-down version of the Argument From Design, reveals a lack of philosophical sophistication:

> But God had created both Man and Nature, placing Man into that Nature as a hand is placed into a glove. Amanda frequently reflected upon the fruits of the field, how various they were, and yet how perfectly each was adapted for Man's enjoyment. For instance, trees bearing edible fruit were made easy to climb, being much lower than forest trees. Fruits which were soft when ripe, such as the apricot, the fig or the mulberry, which might be bruised by falling, presented themselves at a small distance from the ground; whereas hard fruit, which ran no risk of sustaining an injury by a fall, like the cocoa, the walnut or the chestnut, presented themselves at a considerable height. Some fruit—like the cherry and the plum—were moulded for the mouth; others—the apple and the pear—for the hand. (147)

At the beginning of the story, Amanda is seated at the side of her father's death-bed reading "some kind of religious mumbo-jumbo." When she is suddenly distracted by the sound of a beetle chirping on the ceiling (a sound which, as everyone knew, "portended the death of someone in the house within the year"), her father exclaims:

> It's love. . . . That's all it is . . . . It's the love call of *xestobium rufo-villosum* for God's sake, girl. Simple as that. Put one of the little fellows in a box and tap on the table with a pencil and he behaves in exactly the same way. Thinks you're a female and butts his head against the box trying to get to you. (146)

Where Amanda sees matrimonial and family life as an expression of God's benevolent world-plan, Mr. Fergusson's views on the origin of domestic felicity are decidedly more glandular. According to the narrator, Mr. Fergusson could not "quite bear to inform his daughter that the human family sprang from the same impulse which animated a beetle striking its head against the walls of its box. . ." (148).

For Amanda, the "halo" cloud which she and Miss Logan will later see encircling the summit of Mt. Ararat is a sign of the mountain's holiness; but as Amanda informs her friend, the "Colonel" would have explained the appearance of the halo in a different way:

> People like my father would not agree. They would tell us that such comparisons are all hot air. Literally. They would explain that the halo cloud is a perfectly natural phenomenon. During the night and for several hours after dawn the summit remains clearly visible, but as the plain warms up in the morning sun, the hot air rises and becomes vapour at a given height. At the day's end, when everything

cools down again, the halo disappears. It comes as no surprise to . . . science. (154)

To her father, Amanda continues, the halo "would be all vapour and clouds and rising air. . . . But who created the vapour, who created the clouds? Who ensured that Noah's mountain of all mountains would be blessed each day with a halo of cloud?" (154).

In a similar scene in "Project Ararat," the main character, an ex-astronaut named Spike Tiggler, becomes overjoyed when, near the base of Ararat, he sees a stream flowing uphill. When his geologist travelling companion, Dr. Jimmy Fulgood, attempts to offer a scientific explanation of the phenomenon, Spike remains undaunted:

> It depended on a certain weight and pressure of water higher up the mountain, and on the apparently uphill stretch being a comparatively small section of an overall descent. . . . Spike, who was driving, kept nodding away as cheerful as they come. 'Reckon you could explain it like that,' he commented at the end. 'Point is, who made the water to flow uphill in the first place? Who put it where He did so that we should see it as we were passing on the road to Ararat? The Good Lord, that's who. It's the land of miracles,' he repeated, nodding contentedly. (269)

Earlier, when Dr. Fulgood had recommended that Spike use his influence at NASA to get aerial photographs of the mountain, Spike expressed his reservations, wondering "if God had really intended them to take short-cuts. Wasn't the whole vision of the project as a sort of Christian pilgrimage, and didn't the ancient pilgrims always rough it? . . . He did feel they should hope to feel guided by something other than modern technology once they got up there" (266).

In "Project Ararat," Barnes' "fictionalizes" the career of American astronaut James Irwin. The two principal facts around which Barnes constructs (and "fabulates") his story are an actual space mission (Irwin's exploration of the moon in 1975) and a religious "pilgrimage" (the ex-astronaut's expedition to Mt. Ararat in 1985). The story recounts both the early life and the career of Spike Tiggler, Irwin's "fictional counterpart." After growing up in North Carolina, where a brief visit to Kitty Hawk with his father inspired him to pursue a career in aviation, Spike joins the Navy and flies missions in Korea. While it is true that some of the residents of his home town, including the mother of the girl who introduced him to sex, were glad to see Spike go, most of the people of Wadesville remember him as a decent, if somewhat high-spirited, young man whose conduct at times exhibited a healthy adolescent's insouciance toward spiritual matters. As the narrator observes, when Spike departed Wadesville for military service, he had "left his faith behind."

> Though he dutifully filled in 'Baptist' on all the Navy forms, he didn't think about the Lord's commands, or the blessed grace, or being saved, not even on the bad days when one of his fellow aviators—hell, one of his friends—bought the farm. That was a friend gone, but you didn't try to raise the Lord on the radio. Spike was a flier, a man of science, an engineer. You might acknowledge God on a paper form just as you deferred to senior officers around the base; yet the moment you were most you . . . was when you'd climbed hard and were levelling out your silver wings, high up in the clear air south of the Yalu River. (252)

After serving in Korea, Spike becomes a lunar astronaut in the Apollo space program. But when his turn to travel into space finally comes, he has an experience which changes his life forever, transforming the man of science into the man of God. While exploring the surface of the moon, Spike hears a voice in his helmet enjoining him to go "find Noah's Ark." At first, he merely shrugs it off, thinking that the fellows back at Mission Control are playing some kind of joke on him, but when he hears the voice again, he becomes confused and distracted. Back on earth, Spike reflects on his experience and decides that the voice he heard on the moon was God's. But for several months, during which time he is feted from one end of the country to the other for his achievements in space, Spike does not act on God's request. On his way to a special award ceremony which the state of North Carolina has organized for him at Kitty Hawk, Spike spots a giant replica of Noah's Ark on the side of the road. Convinced that this simulacrum, which serves, appropriately, as a worship center, is God's way of reminding him to pursue his quest for the real Ark, Spike finally confides in his wife Betty about what had happened to him on the moon:

> I didn't tell anyone. I know I'm not hallucinating. I know I've heard what I've heard, but I don't tell. Maybe I'm not quite sure, maybe I want to forget it. And what happens? The very day I go back to Kitty Hawk, where it all started all those years ago, the very day I go back I see the God-damn Ark. Don't forget about what I said—that's His message, isn't it? Loud and clear. That's what it means. Go ahead and get your medal, but don't forget what I said. (255)

Not long after this, Spike begins to display signs which alarm his wife (who, having eagerly looked forward to the large revenues from her husband's anticipated commercial endorsements, lectures, and television appearances, laments the fact that he has fallen off the "box car of the gravy train"). First, Spike announces that he is leaving the space program;

shortly after that he resigns his commission from the Navy. Meanwhile, Betty has begun to worry about what other people might be thinking about her husband's increasing pensiveness and his reclusive lifestyle (he spends all day in his backyard reading the Bible and gazing up at the sky).

No sooner is Betty ready to have her husband committed, than Spike announces his plan to organize an expedition to Mt. Ararat. After crisscrossing the state of North Carolina to raise the necessary funds (in his fund-raising speeches, especially the one he makes in Wadesville, he always talks about the idea of "escape and return" and of the importance of going back to one's beginnings—a theme which will resonate throughout the story), Spike assembles the expeditionary team. Besides himself, he enlists Betty for her sharp business acumen, Reverend Lance Gibson for spiritual guidance, and Dr. Jimmy Fulgood for his expertise in geology. As in "The Mountain," however, only two people actually make the journey to Ararat: Spike, whose religious fervor recalls that of Amanda, and Jimmy, whose scientific temperament and occasional puzzlement over the veracity of Scriptural anecdote liken him both to Colonel Fergusson and Miss Logan. And like the earlier story, "Project Ararat" features the same interplay between dogged faith and nudging doubt. This tug-of-war can be seen in the conversation which Spike and Jimmy Fulgood have when they first see Great and Little Ararat. Spike's opening comment recalls Amanda's thoughts as she first looked upon the pair of mountains nearly 130 years earlier:

> 'Kinda like man and wife, aint it?' Spike remarked.
> 'How d'ya mean?'
> 'Brother and sister, Adam and Eve. The big one there and the little neat pretty one by his side. See? Male and Female created He them.
> 'Do you think the Lord had that in mind at the time?'
> 'The Lord has everything in mind,' said Spike Tiggler. 'All the time.' Jimmy Fulgood looked at the twin shapes ahead of them and kept to himself the reflection that Betty Tiggler was an inch or two taller than Spike. (270)

"Project Ararat" and "The Mountain" intersect in other significant ways as well. For instance, before leaving, the men collect all the necessary equipment, just as their female counterparts had done in "The Mountain." Like Amanda and Miss Logan, moreover, Spike and his companion remember to include presents for their Turkish hosts. And just as the two women before them had brought bottles to collect the "unfermented" juice of Noah's grapes (they actually end up filling them with snow from the mountain), so Spike takes along bottles which will be filled with the "holy" waters of Ararat's streams. What is more, Spike's refusal to bring his bottle of whiskey up onto Noah's "holy" mountain echoes Amanda's refusal to drink the wine from Noah's vineyards.

The two main characters also evince a similar inflexibility of mind where matters of theology and scripture are concerned. For instance, we have already noted Amanda's antipathy toward not only science but also Islam and the "corruptions" of the Eastern Christian Church. In "Project Ararat," Spike and Jimmy puzzle over the theological implications of the Soviet Union's claiming one-third of Ararat for itself:

> 'Doesn't seem right, the Soviets having a piece of it,' commented Jimmy.
> 'Guess they weren't Soviets at the time,' said Spike.
> 'They were Christians like us when they were just Russians.'
> 'Mebbe the Lord took their slice of the mountain away from them when they became Soviets.'
> 'Mebbe,' replied Spike, not wholly certain of when the boundaries had shifted.
> 'Like, not letting his holy mountain fall into the hands of the infidels.'
> 'I read you,' said Spike, a little irritated. 'But I guess the Turks aren't exactly Christians.'
> 'They're not as infidel as the Soviets.' Jimmy appeared reluctant to give up his theory at the first objection.
> 'Check.' (268–269)

Later, Spike tells his companion about the earthquake of 1840 and its destruction of the village of Arghuri, including the Monastery of St. James (the very event which Amanda and Miss Logan witnessed from the slopes of Ararat). To Spike, the quake, which had "gotten hold of the mountain and shaken it like a dog with a rat," was "like the vengeance of the Lord" (268). Meanwhile, Jimmy, infected perhaps by his companion's zeal,

> nodded seriously to himself as he listened to the story. All this had happened, he told himself, at a time when the Soviets had owned this slice of the mountain. Of course they were Russians then, and Christian, but it proved the Lord sure did have it in for the Soviets, even before they were Soviets. (271–272)

Finally, Spike and Jimmy not only discover the "gently sloping valley" in which Amanda believed the Ark had come to rest, but also remark the halo of cloud around the mountain's summit and the strange green coloring of the sky above the peak which had moved Amanda to declare Ararat a "holy" mountain. Ironically, the narrator of "Project Ararat" describes the formation of the "halo" in scientific terms:

> Each day, as the sun heated up the plain below them and the warm air rose, a halo of cloud formed itself around the mountaintop, shutting off their view of the lower slopes; and each night, as the air cooled, the cloud dispersed. (272)

As for the exploration itself, the men make three unsuccessful forays onto the mountain. On their third try they discover the very same caves that Miss Logan had laid her injured companion in. In one of the caves, Spike discovers a human skeleton which he presumes to be Noah's. After supper that evening, Spike goes back into the cave to check on the bones. As he re-emerges he sees a full moon (recalling the moon which Amanda looked at from the cave) and reports that "the position of the skeleton would have allowed the dying Noah to gaze out fom the cave and see the moon—the very moon on whose surface Spike Tiggler had so recently stood" (274).

However, later that evening, Jimmy Fulgood voices his concerns about the identity of the skeleton:

> 'Spike, those bones in the cave—don't they . . . don't they look a little, how shall I put it, well-preserved? I mean, I'm only playing Devil's advocate, you understand.'
> 'Relax, Jimmy, you're doing fine.'
> 'But they do look well-preserved.' (274-275)

Jimmy's doubts eventually prevail over Spike, and he agrees to submit the bones to a carbon dating test. When the results arrive from Washington, they reveal that the skeleton is approximately 150 years old and is "almost certainly that of a woman." At the end of the story, Spike is back at the Moondust Diner in Wadesville, "announcing the launch of the Second Project Ararat."

VII

Barnes' next chapter, "Three Simple Stories," contains three short narratives on widely disparate subjects. Ranging over the worlds of biblical lore and historical fact, the chapter includes a re-telling of the Jonah myth; a short narrative about James Beesley, the *Titanic* survivor who later described his experiences in *The Loss of the Titanic*; and an account of the voyage of the *St. Louis*, the German ocean liner which in 1939, while carrying a cargo of 930 Jewish refugees seeking political asylum, was turned away, first by Cuba, then by the United States, and finally by several European nations.

The first story, a grimly humorous variation on a theme we encountered in "Shipwreck"—how catastrophe is turned into art—illustrates what the narrator refers to as "Marx's elaboration of Hegel: history repeats itself, the first time as tragedy, the second time as farce" (175). The story

A History of the World in 10 1/2 Chapters 93

is narrated by an eighteen-year-old English lad who spends a summer tutoring at a prep school. The school's founder, Lawrence Beesley, is the author of *The Loss of the Titanic*, a book which was based on his eyewitness account of the disaster in 1912. Owing to the book's enormous popularity, Beesley was "regularly consulted by maritime historians, film researchers, journalists, souvenir hunters, bores, and vexatious litigants," not to mention "newsmen eager for him to imagine the fate of the victims" of other ships sunk by icebergs.

In the course of his short stay at the school, the narrator, equipped with a veritable arsenal of precocious insights into life's evils and injustices, discovers things about Mr. Beesley's conduct aboard the imperilled *Titanic* which merely verify his already less than optimistic view of human nature. According to what he is able to glean from the rumors and innuendoes circulated by the venerable old schoolmaster's own family members, the narrator learns that Mr. Beesley survived the *Titanic* disaster by impersonating a woman—a "hypothesis" which seemed to be confirmed by the fact that Beesley's name never appeared on the official list of the ship's survivors. As the narrator says:

> I supported this theory with pleaure, because it confirmed my view of the world. In the autumn of that year I was to wedge into the mirror of my college bedsitting-room a piece of paper bearing the following lines: 'Life's a cheat and all things shew it/I thought so once and now I know it.' Beesley's case offered corroboration: the hero of the *Titanic* was a blanket-forger and transvestite imposter. (173–174)

From this point on, the story thematizes what might be referred to as the ontology of fictional representation and the relationship between art and life. For instance, the narrator also learns (this time from Beesley's daughter) that many years later, when *A Night To Remember*, the film version of *The Loss of the Titanic*, was being made, the author was hired as a consultant. According to his daughter, Beesley was captivated by the artificial staging of the disaster, particularly by the miniature replica of the ship and the "ruckled black velvet" material which was used to represent the sea. Moreover, he was "keen to be among the extras who despairingly crowded the rail as the ship went down—keen, you could say, to undergo in fiction an alternative version of history" (174). When the director attempts to prevent Beesley from doing this by invoking union regulations, the ex-*Titanic* survivor forges a union card and assumes a disguise (he dons a period costume). But just before shooting commences, the director manages to ferret Beesley out again and orders him off the set: "And so, for the second time in his life, Lawrence Beesley found himself leaving the *Titanic* just before it was due to go down" (175).

In the second story of the triptych, Barnes explores the relation of myth to reality. In it, the author re-tells the story of Jonah and the whale and offers a number of reasons to explain man's collective fascination with the myth. Indeed, so engrossing is this story that among painters, for instance, Jonah's and the whale's popularity exceeds even that of Noah; for whereas the narrator of "Shipwreck" had spoken of the dearth of "Noah"/"Ark" paintings in Western Art, the narrator in this story quips that "Jonah (depicted as everything from muscular faun to bearded elder) has an iconography whose pedigree and variety would make Noah envious" (177).

To the narrator, who once panicked when—while travelling from London to Paris—he found himself in "the locked sleeping compartment of a locked coach in a locked hold beneath the waterline on a cross-channel ferry" (178), one reason for the story's riveting hold on audiences is its promise of spiritual deliverance:

> the proof that there is salvation and justice after our purgatorial incarceration. Like Jonah, we are all storm-tossed on the seas of life, undergo apparent death and certain burial, but then attain a blinding resurrection as the car-ferry doors swing open and we are delivered back into the light and into the recognition of God's love. (178)

Not surprisingly, however, most of the reasons have to do with fear: fear of being swallowed, of suffocating, of being buried alive, of going back to the womb. The narrator concedes that, although God is a sloppy story writer (and here Barnes may be playing with the Romantic notion of the writer as God-Figure), His choice of a whale (or giant fish as some would have it) to inspire fear is uncanny:

> Technically, the cetacean side of things isn't at all well-handled: the beast is evidently as much of a pawn as Jonah; its providential appearance just as the sailors are tossing Jonah overboard smacks far too heavily of a *deus ex machina*; and the great fish is casually dismissed from the story the moment its narrative function has been fulfilled. . . . God finger-flips the blubbery jail hither and thither like a war-game admiral nudging his fleet across maps of the sea.
> And yet, despite all this, the whale steals it. We forget the allegorical point of the story (Babylon engulfing disobedient Israel), we don't much care whether or not Nineveh was saved, or what happened to the regurgitated penitent; but we remember the whale. (177)

The narrator likens the story's "fear-effect" to that of Peter Benchley's *Jaws*. According to novelist Kingsley Amis, whom the narrator quotes,

Jaws is about "being bloody frightened of being eaten by a bloody big shark" (178).

> At bottom, this is the grip which the story of Jonah and the whale still has on us: fear of being devoured by a large creature, fear of being chomped, slurped, gargled, washed down with a draught of salt water and a school of anchovies as a chaser . . . fear of sensory deprivation, which we know drives people mad. (178)

It is also apparent, however, that much of this fear is instilled by God Himself, thus further expanding the theme of ruthless authority which underlies many of the stories in *A History*. As in "The Stowaway," where God is referred to as Noah's "oppressive role-model," the God in "Jonah" is characterized as a power-hungry tyrant, whose creation (at least as it is delineated in the stories of the Old Testament) exhibits a "crippling lack of free will . . . or even the illusion of free will. God holds all the cards and wins all the tricks" (176). The God who terrorizes Jonah into preaching against the iniquities of Nineveh, we recall, is the same Deity who "finger-flips" His subjects around the globe like a "war-game admiral nudging his fleet across maps of the sea" (177).

Having both uncovered the story's archetypal thematic structures and exposed God as a "paranoid schizophrenic" and "moral bully," the narrator next ponders the problem of plausibility. How can twentieth-century man, endowed with all the sophistication necessary to distinguish reality from myth, be taken in by such a story? Enlisting the aid of modern scientific research, the narrator initially argues that no human being could possibly survive ingestion by a whale. But, as if to belie the evidence of science, he then cites the "actual" case of James Bartley, a sailor who by his own account, as well as by the eyewitness testimony of others, was swallowed by a whale in 1891. Bartley, who was extracted from the whale's stomach several hours after the animal was killed by the hapless seaman's shipmates, lived to write about his experience. The sailor's adventure confirms the narrator's view that reality follows myth—that the "myth of Bartley" was "begotten by the myth of Jonah." For the narrator, the point of this strange juxtaposition of myth and reality is

> not that myth refers us back to some original event which has been fancifully transcribed as it passed through the collective memory; but that it refers us forward to something that will happen. Myth will become reality, however sceptical we may be. (181)

As we have seen, *A History of the World in 10 1/2 Chapters* contains several stories which feature sea voyagers in danger: the animals on Noah's Ark in "The Stowaway"; the tourist-hostages in "The Visitors";

Kath Ferris alone on the Pacific Ocean in "The Survivor"; the castaways on the raft of the *Medusa* in "Shipwreck"; and Jonah in the central triptych of "Three Simple Stories." In the third section of Chapter 17, Barnes turns his attention to one of human history's most catastrophic events—the Jewish Holocaust. Told in an almost flat documentary style, the story, which recounts the infamous voyage of the German ocean liner *St. Louis*, is nevertheless a compelling evocation of human venality, hypocrisy, and injustice.

Carrying 931 Jewish "refugees," the *St. Louis* left Hamburg, Germany for Cuba on May 13, 1939. In spite of all that the Jews had been through in the weeks and months prior to embarking, the mood aboard ship as it steamed toward Cuba and the promise of freedom was jubilant. As Barnes observes: "Perhaps their escape from Germany felt as miraculous as that of Jonah from the whale" (182). However, upon its arrival at Havana on May 27, the Cuban government refused to admit the refugees. Shortly after the ship's departure from Germany the president of Cuba, presumably hoping to extort as much money from the ill-fated Jews as he could, had rescinded the disembarkation certificates. Incredibly, bribes were offered—the initial price being set at $500.00 per Jew.

The Joint Distribution Committee, a Jewish relief organization, interceded on behalf of the refugees and began negotiations with the Cuban authorities. But when the talks broke down, the President of Cuba ordered the *St. Louis* to leave Havana. As the captain of the ship turned his vessel northward, confident that The United States would accept the Jews, negotiations were resumed in Cuba—in which several different "disembarkation fees" were put forth, the highest reaching one million dollars for the entire boatload. This figure was eventually reduced to $453, 500, and the Cuban officials wired the captain to return his ship to Havana. Their hopes buoyed up for a second time, the Jews began to prepare for disembarkation. However, when a last minute hitch in this second round of negotiations could not be resolved, the *St. Louis* was again ordered to turn away from Cuba.

The ship steamed northward for a second time. Somewhere near the coast of Florida it was intercepted by a United States Coast Guard vessel and turned away from American shores. At this point a passenger committee aboard the *St. Louis* began dispatching cables to prominent citizens and political figures in The United States and Latin America pleading for their intercession. By and large, these messages went unanswered. Meanwhile, the *St. Louis'* captain had been considering desperate measures to attract world attention to the plight of his passengers, including setting fire to his ship in the hope that the rescuing nation would feel compelled to offer the Jews safe haven. When this plan was rejected, the passengers, the captain, and the shipping line continued to broadcast their now international plea for assistance.

History blames Nazi Germany for the Jewish Holocaust, but Barnes' re-telling of the plight of the *St. Louis* reminds us that the whole world must bear the responsibility for the Holocaust, not just Germany. To that extent, Barnes' treatment of the story exemplifies postmodernist literature's concern with the "truthfulness" of history, as well as with the need to "revise" previously unchallenged versions of history. As the story of the *St. Louis* reveals, country after country, including The United States and several South and Central American nations, refused to admit the Jews. *Der Sturmer*, a German newspaper, announced that "if the Jews chose to take up their return passages to Germany, they should be accommodated at Dachau and Buchenwald" (184). As Barnes points out, harboring the Jews was apparently perceived by the potential host country as a political liability:

> Meanwhile, in Havana harbour, American reporters managed to get on board what they nicknamed, perhaps too easily, 'the ship that shamed the world.' Such publicity does not necessarily help refugees. If the shame belongs to the whole world, then why should one particular country—which had already accepted many Jewish refugees—be so frequently expected to bear it? (184–185)

England and France were soon approached: "The British answer was that they would prefer to view the present difficulty in the wider context of the general European refugee situation, but that they might be prepared to consider possible subsequent entry of the Jews to Britain after their return to Germany" (187). Later, German radio made great play of the world's bogus concern for the Jews. One station announced that

> since no country would agree to accept the boat-load of Jews, the Fatherland would be obliged to take them back and support them. It was not difficult to imagine where they might be supported. What's more, if the *St. Louis* was forced to unload its cargo of degenerates and criminals back in Hamburg, this would prove that the world's supposed concern was mere hypocrisy. Nobody wanted the shabby Jews, and nobody therefore had any right to criticize whatever welcome the Fatherland might extend to the filthy parasites on their return. (187)

The Jews' hopes for a bright future—indeed, for any future—plummeted when the captain, having exhausted every possible course of action, turned his ship eastward toward Europe. However, a breakthrough came several days later. Belgium suddenly announced that it would accept 200 of the ship's Jews. Holland, Britain, and France soon followed

Belgium's lead, agreeing to receive 194, 350, and 250 passengers respectively. Tragically, after the outbreak of war in September 1939, many of the refugees eventually ended up in concentration camps anyway. Those who were lucky enough to have been chosen by England, and later The United States, survived. When the *St. Louis'* "British contingent" landed at Southhampton on June 21st, its members "were able to reflect that their wanderings at sea had lasted precisely forty days and forty nights" (189). Once again, myth had become reality.

VIII

Barnes' next story, "Upstream!", is presented in a series of letters written by the main character—a British TV and movie star known only as Charlie in the story—to his estranged girlfriend back in London. The story takes place in a remote area in the jungles of South America, where a film about two Catholic missionaries who had explored that region some two or three hundred years earlier is being shot. In the movie, Charlie is playing the role of Father Firmin, a stern, authoritarian Jesuit priest who is opposed to baptizing the Indians; while his co-star, an abrasive, egocentric American actor named Matt, is impersonating Firmin's more moderate and open-minded colleague, Father Antonio, who favors converting the natives. During filming the two actors constantly lock horns over role priority (just as the "historical" figures they are impersonating had squared-off over the matter of converting the natives). To Charlie,

> Matt is not exactly the most spiritual and sophisticated fellow you've ever met. Believes in making your own way through life, walking tall, shooting straight, balling chicks as he puts it and spitting in the eye of anyone who does you wrong. That at any rate seems to be the sum of his wisdom. He thinks the Indians are rather cute kids who haven't yet invented the video recorder. I must say it's pretty funny that a chap like him ends up playing a Jesuit priest having doctrinal disputes in the rain forest. The fact is, he's one of those perfectly efficient American actors whose careers are decided by their image makers. (204).

The rest of the cast consists of the Indians who have been hired as "extras" to perform essentially the same tasks as their ancestors did. As Charlie reflects on this strange bit of historical *deja vu*, he wonders if the tribesmen had "ballads about transporting the two white men dressed as women up to the great watery Anaconda to the south? . . . Or did the white men vanish from the tribe's memory as completely as the tribe vanished from the white man?" (201).

One of the story's main themes is the contrast between "primitive man" and "civilized man." Initially intrigued by the natives' simplicity, their innate dignity (they do not prostrate themselves before the "civilized" white men; nor do they seem particularly impressed by all the gadgets of modern technology), and their pristine ingenuousness, Charlie claims that his exposure to the Indians has dramatically changed his perspective on civilized life. In a passage which anticipates "Project Ararat," Charlie likens his experience in the jungle to that of the astronauts on the moon:

> It's something about being here. You remember the American astronauts, how they went to the moon and came back totally changed by looking at the earth and seeing it just like any old planet all small and a long way away? Some of them got religious or went barmy I seem to remember, but the point is they were all different when they came back. It's a bit like that with me, except that instead of going into the future I had to go back in time. (200)

Charlie marvels at the fact that the natives have no name for themselves (thus reflecting, so he believes, a complete absence of ethnocentricity) and apparently feel, like Jonathan Swift's Houyhnhnms, no need to deceive, although they are not averse to playing practical jokes (most of which revolve around their words for human reproductive organs) on the main character. When the members of the film crew somewhat contemptuously remark the Indians' ignorance of such modern technological wonders as the radio, the protagonist replies, "I think they're fantastically advanced and mature because they don't have the radio" (200).

Charlie's jungle "odyssey" gives him ample opportunity to reflect on the pitfalls of twentieth-century urban life. In a letter in which he attempts to apologize for a recent affair he had with a woman named Linda, Charlie writes:

> ... but it's all to do with London isn't it? Not really to do with us at all. Just bloody London with its grime and filthy streets and the booze. Well, that's not really living, the way we do in the cities, is it? Also I think cities make people lie to one another. Do you think that's possible? These Indians never lie, same as they don't know how to act. No pretense. Now I don't think that's primitive at all, I think it's bloody mature. And I'm sure it's because they live in the jungle not in cities. They spend all their time surrounded by nature, and the one thing nature doesn't do is lie. It just goes ahead and does its thing, as Matt would say. Walks tall and shoots straight. It may not be nice some of the time but it doesn't lie. (205)

In another letter, Charlie informs his girlfriend of his intention, upon returning to England, of decamping London and moving into the country, where they will raise a child, for whom Charlie will "make a playpen" and "buy one of those big wooden Arks with all the animals in" (206).

But "Upstream!" also contains details which seem to undermine the "Tropical Paradise " theme, and which open up the possibility that Barnes may be parodying literary works which, by privileging the values of primitive society over those of the civilized world, popularized the Romantic idea of the "Noble Savage." For example, when the main character first meets the tribe, he is impressed by the natives' robust nakedness and apparent good health, while at the same time puzzling over the absence of elderly Indians. Later, he learns that the natives do not live past the age of 35. In his letter home, Charlie admits that "I was wrong when I thought they were fantastically healthy and a good advert for the Jungle. The truth is it's only the fantastically healthy ones who can get by at all. What a turnaround" (205).

Charlie is also surprised when, in another scene, the natives fail to mourn the death of one of their tribesmen (he had fallen into the river and drowned while rafting the crew upriver)—a failure which, for Charlie, seems to reveal a lack of emotional sensitivity. Earlier, Charlie had found himself in the middle of an incident which seemed to reveal the Indians' racial "snobbery." One evening, as they prepare to settle in for the night, the party (including the men and women of the tribe) split into two separate camps—one for the white men and one for the Indians. When Charlie, who feels somewhat awkward with this arrangement, attempts to "desegregate" the camps, he finds that "some of of the crew were against this because they thought they'd get their watches stolen. . .and some were in favor so that they could get a closer look at the women" (198). Meanwhile, the crew's translator, who had been sent to the Indian camp to help ease tensions between the two groups, returns to inform the white men that the natives have no desire to share their camp with them.

The final shock to Charles comes when he learns that the natives, whom he suddenly refers to as "those fucking Indians" in one of his letters, have not only caused Matt's death but also stolen food, clothing, and much of the crew's film equipment.

Like many postmodernist fictional narratives,"Upstream!" features a Chinese-box structure, wherein a fictitious series of letters is used to recount the making of a fictitious film in which fictitious actors impersonate figures whose own historicity, though purportedly real, is just as fictitious as that of the "actors" who portray them in the film (Fathers Firmin and Antonio were not actual historical persons, but rather characters in a fictional story, part of whose purpose is to convince us that the two priests actually did live at one time). Thus, just as the narrative's "epistolary" frame helps lend authenticity to the events being recounted (perhaps because we tend to believe in the autobiographical veracity of letters), so Barnes' use of cinema allows him to thematize the conflict between illusion and reality.

Distinguishing the actual "historical" missionaries—both of whom had nearly drowned when the raft that was taking them upriver capsized—from the actors who impersonate the missionaries on film proves to be a particularly thorny problem for the native Indians hired as "extras" by the film crew. Unable to comprehend the concept of "acting," the Indians, whose job it is to paddle the "priests" upstream—just as their real-life ancestors had done two or three centuries before—fail to differentiate between the "real" missionaries and the actors who are playing those roles in front of the camera.

At first, Charlie merely notes the strange recurrence of events:

> It's amazing when you think about it. Here's this tribe, totally obscure, don't even have a name for themselves. A couple of hundred years ago two Jesuit missionaries trying to find their way back to the Orinoco stumble across them, get them to build a raft and then pole the two Godmen several hundred miles south while the said Godmen preach them the Gospel and try to get them to wear Levis. Just when they get near their destination the raft capsizes, the missionaries nearly drown and the Indians disappear. . . . Now they're helping us do exactly the same thing a couple of hundred years on. (201)

But Charlie's later observations of the Indians' reactions to movie-making go right to the heart of filmic representation. To the Indians, the two white men who dress in missionary robes and recite lines in front of a large glass eye are not actors at all, but the actual missionaries themselves:

> Here's a funny thing. While the Indians appear to understand roughly what we're doing—they're happy to do retakes and don't seem at all put out by this great big eye being pointed at them—they don't seem to understand about the idea of acting. I mean sure they're acting their ancestors and they're quite willing . . . to build us a raft and transport us upstream on it and be filmed doing this. But they won't do anything else. If Vic says could you stand in a different way or use the pole like this and tries to demonstrate they simply won't. Absolutely refuse. This is how we pole a raft and just because a white man is watching through his funny machine we aren't going to do it differently. The other thing is even more incredible. They actually think that when Matt and I are dressed up as Jesuits we actually are Jesuits! They think we've gone away and these two blokes in black dresses have turned up! Father Firmin is just as real a person for them as Charlie. . . . the crew think this is pretty stupid of them but I wonder if it isn't fantastically mature. The crew think they're such a primitive civilization that they haven't discovered acting yet. I wonder if it's the opposite and they're a sort of

post-acting civilization. . . . Like they don't need it any more, so they've forgotten about it and don't understand it any longer. (202–203)

As the work on the set becomes more intensive, Charlie feels that fiction is beginning to encroach upon reality:

> The film is spilling over into the rest of the time. Even the Indians don't seem so sure that I'm not Firmin all the time and Matt's Antonio. It's as if they think I'm really Firmin and then from time to time I just pretend to be this white man called Charlie. Really upside down. (208)

Thus, when it comes time to film a scene in which Father Antonio, who is still arguing with Father Firmin over the baptism of the natives, "semi-accidentally" hits his superior with a paddle (made of balsa wood), the Indians, not realizing that it is all an illusion, rush to Father Firmin's assistance as if he had actually been injured:

> The Indians were supposed to look on at what was happening as if these two white men in skirts were barmy. That's what they'd been told to do. But they didn't. Lots of them came rushing over to me and started stroking my face and wetting my brow and making a sort of wailing noise, and then three of them turned on Matt looking really nasty. Incredible! What's more they might have done him an injury if he hadn't pulled off his hassock pretty smartish and turned back into Matt, which calmed them down. Amazing! It was only old Matt, and that nasty priest Antonio had gone away. (206–207)

The relationship between fiction and reality is given further ironical play in the film's climactic scene—the capsizing of the raft. The shooting of the scene, which occurs over a three day period, requires the use of safety ropes (ropes which may recall the tow-lines attached to the "machine" in "Shipwreck") to secure both the raft (to a tree on shore) and the actors, and special-effects equipment to create the illusion of turbulent white-water rapids. Hoping to allay any possible fears that his girlfriend may have about the safety of the scene, Charlie, like many good postmodernists, simultaneously reveals the fiction-making processes of his art:

> Don't worry darling it's not really dangerous. We're doing some covering footage on a stretch of the river where there are some rapids, but the actual capsizing which is meant to happen there doesn't really. The crew have got a couple of machines which churn everything up to make white water and the chippie ran up some rocks which they anchor to the bottom of the river and look just like the real thing. (209–210)

After the raft turns over, the scene calls for Father Antonio to save Father Firmin. But just as they prepare for the final shooting of the scene, Charlie and Matt notice that there are only two Indians poling the raft, instead of the required twelve. Before they know it, the raft is breaking loose into the rapids and going over. With great difficulty Charlie manages to swim to the shore, but Matt disappears. Hoping to find him "clinging to the branches of trees overhanging the river downstream," the men on shore race along the river banks. But as Charlie points out in a passage which ironically reflects on the relation of illusion to reality and the nature of film art: "it wasn't like that. That sort of thing is strictly for the movies. Matt was gone . . ." (215). With the exception of Matt's death, then, the movie version of the accident ironically ends up duplicating the "historical" capsizing.

Charlie and the other crew members become suspicious when, while examining the tree which the safety rope was supposed to be tied to, they discover that the rope is gone. This, together with the under-manned raft, the theft of the supplies, and the sudden disappearance of the Indians, apparently convinces some of the men that the natives had schemed to rob the crew right from the beginning. But Charlie offers two other explanations for the "mis-hap," each one underscoring the interplay between art and life. According to one of his theories, the Indians realized that Matt and Charlie were arguing about converting them,

> and at the point the raft capsized it looked as if I [Charlie] was winning the argument. I was the senior priest, after all, and I was against baptism. . . . So maybe the Indians understood this and tipped up the raft because they were trying to kill Father Firmin (me!) so that Father Antonio would survive and baptise them. (217)

But when the Indians see that Father Firmin has survived and Antonio drowned, they flee in fear.

In his second explanation, Charlie theorizes that the Indians were frightened because they knew the story of the two Jesuit missionaries and did not want to witness the capsizing:

> It seems to me that the Indians—our Indians—knew what had happened to Father Firmin and Father Antonio all those years ago. . . . Those Jesuits were probably quite big in the Indians' history. Think of that story getting passed down the generations, each time they handed it on it became more colorful and exaggerated. And then we come along, another lot of white men who've also got two chaps in long black skirts with them, who also want to be poled up the river to the Orinoco. Sure there are differences, they've got this one-eyed machine and so on, but basically it's the same thing, and we even tell them it's going to end in the same way with the raft capsizing. (216–217)

As Charlie later observes, what the natives presumably felt they were witnessing was not the fictional re-creation of historical events but rather a case of history merely repeating itself, and in an ironical way he is absolutely right: on two separate occasions, a pair of white men wearing long black robes appear in the jungle, argue over the spiritual status of the natives, and, while being "poled" upstream to the Orinoco, get thrown into the river when their raft capsizes.

IX

"Parenthesis," the only unnumbered chapter in the book (presumably this is the "1/2 chapter" of the title), brings together themes and motifs from several of the other stories in *A History*. This reprising of elements from the earlier narratives (there is one proleptical reference to "Project Ararat"), not only recapitulates the development of *A History*'s underlying theme of recurrent human catastrophe but also allows Barnes to express his impatience with man's inability and/or unwillingness to learn from history. For instance, in a passage which recalls both the brutality aboard Noah's Ark and the acts of cannibalism on the raft of the *Medusa* in "Shipwreck," Barnes speaks of the need to teach love (not just sex education) in schools so that young people will not have to depend solely on "Nature" as a guide in their romantic relationships:

> Trusting virgins drafted into marriage never found Nature had all the answers when they turned out the light. Trusting virgins were told that love was the promised land, an ark on which two might escape the Flood. It may be an ark, but one on which anthrophophagy is rife; an ark skippered by some crazy greybeard who beats you round the head with his gopher-wood stave, and might pitch you overboard at any moment. (229)

In another passage the narrator, who identifies himself as Julian Barnes, relates how "The Armenians believed Mt. Ararat was the centre of the world, but the mountain was divided between three great empires, and the Armenians ended up with none of it" (234)—a statement which recalls both "The Mountain" and "Project Ararat." Later, in a section which harks back to "The Survivor," Barnes writes:

> We get scared by history; we allow ourselves to be bullied by dates.
>   In fourteen hundred and ninety-two
>   Columbus sailed the ocean blue.
> And then what? Everyone became wiser? People stopped building new ghettoes in which to practice the old persecutions? Stopped making the old mistakes, or new mistakes, or new versions of old mistakes? (239)

Other connections to "The Survivor" include (1) Barnes' description of contemporary man as hospital patient "with a bubble of news drip-fed into [his] arm" (240) (recalling Kath Ferris' supposed hospitalization in a psychiatric institution); and (2) his reference to "fabulation":

> And while we fret and writhe in bandaged uncertainty—are we a volunatry patient?—we fabulate. We make up a story to cover the facts we don't know or can't accept; we keep a few facts and spin a new story round them. Our panic and pain are only eased by soothing fabulation; we call it history. (240)

A further reference to "The Survivor," as well as to other stories in *A History* ("Shipwreck" and the Lawrence Beesley narrative in "Three Simple Stories") can be found in a passage in which Barnes marvels at history's incredible ability to find things:

> We try to cover them up, but history doesn't let go. However ferociously we ink over our first thoughts, history finds a way of reading them. We bury our victims in secrecy (strangled princelings, irradiated reindeer), but history discovers what we did to them. We lost the *Titanic*, forever it seemed, in the squid-ink depths, but they turned it up. They found the wreck of the *Medusa* not long ago, off the coast of Mauretania. (240-241)

In a subsequent passage, which recalls both "the Stowaway" and Colonel Fergusson in "The Mountain," Barnes elucidates the "materialist" theory of love, according to which,

> Love boils down to pheromones. . . . This bounding of the heart, this clarity of vision, this energizing, this moral certainty, this exaltation, this civic virtue, this murmured I love you, are all caused by a low-level smell emitted by one partner and subconsciously noted by the other. We are just a grander version of that beetle bashing its head in a box at the sound of a tapped pencil. (243)

Finally, in a section which echoes both "The Stowaway" and "The Wars of Religion," Barnes likens the gradual erosion of happiness which many couples experience to the damage which comes "when the woodworm has been gnawing away for years and the bishop's throne collapses" (243).

"Parenthesis" is a meditation on love and its place in human history. As he lies in bed beside his sleeping lover, Barnes reflects that love "gives us our humanity, and also our mysticism" (243). Though it does not guarantee our happiness, love makes us more truthful and clear-sighted; moreover, since it cannot exist without "imaginative sympathy"—the ability to see things from another individual's point of view—love heightens our "civic virtue," making us better citizens. Furthermore, in a passage which echoes D.H. Lawrence, Barnes suggests that love opposes all those forces which threaten to negate life. As he observes, "Love is anti-mechanical, anti-materialist: that's why bad love is still good love. It may make us unhappy, but it insists that the mechanical and the material needn't be in charge" (242).

Agreeing with the spirit, if not altogether with the "logic," of W.H. Auden's line "We must love one another or die," (from "September 1, 1939"), Barnes posits love as an antidote to history. In a passage whose references to "the history of the world" and "half-houses" hint at the book's title, Barnes urges us to love

> Because the history of the world, which only stops at the halfhouse of love to bulldoze it into rubble, is ridiculous without it. The history of the world becomes brutally self-important without love. . . . Love won't change the history of the world . . . but it will do something much more important: teach us to stand up to history, to ignore its chin-out strut. I don't accept your terms, love says; sorry, you don't impress, and by the way what a silly uniform you're wearing. (238)

As presented in "Parenthesis," Barnes' view of history seems to coincide with those of Linda Hutcheon and Hayden White, two critical theorists who have written extensively on the relationship between fiction and historiography. For Barnes, "History isn't what happened. History is just what historians tell us" (240). In *A Poetics of Postmodernism*, Linda Hutcheon argues that historical events are never directly experienced; they can only be known through what she refers to as discursive "traces," the various forms of textual documentation. Speaking of historiographic metafiction, she writes that this genre "demands of the reader not only the recognition of textualized traces of the literary and historical past but also the awareness of what has been done—through irony—to those traces" (127). And she adds that "The reader is forced to acknowledge not only the inevitable textuality of our knowledge of the past, but also both the value and the limitation of the inescapably discursive form of that knowledge" (127).

In his *Tropics of Discourse*, Hayden White writes that "in general there has been a reluctance to consider historical narratives as what they most manifestly are: verbal fictions, the contents of which are as much invented as found and the forms of which have more in common with their counterparts in literature than they have with those in the sciences" (82). White theorizes that historiography is essentially a narrative art and as such, susceptible to all the methods and elements of fictive structuration. According to White, one narrative device common to both historiographer and novelist is plotting. To the extent that he utilizes emplotment strategies in order to impose meaning on his subject matter, the writer of historical narrative participates in a fiction-making activity. In a sense the generic form which the historiographer employs to shape his material into coherent patterns of meaning is itself the "fiction."

Moreover, since he must "familiarize" his contemporary reader with events which time and disparate cultural traditions have rendered "strange" or "exotic," the historiographer finds himself relying on the use of figurative language. For White,

> The historian's characteristic instrument of encodation, communication, and exhange is ordinary educated speech. This implies that the only instruments that he has for endowing his data with meanings, of rendering the strange familiar, and of rendering the mysterious past comprehensible are the techniques of figurative language. (94)

Contrary to conventional wisdom, "meaning" is not an intrinsic component of historical events, but rather something that the historian establishes through his or her use of metaphor, metonymy, synecdoche, and irony (95). In White's words:

> The shape of the relationship which will appear to be inherent in the objects inhabiting the field will in reality have been imposed on the field by the investigator in the very act of identifying and describing the objects that he finds there. The implication is that historians constitute their subjects as possible objects of narrative representation by the very language they use to describe them. (95)

Similarly, Barnes views history as a "pattern, a plan, a movement, expansion, the march of democracy; it is a tapestry, a flow of events, a complex narrative" (240). In history, he adds, "One good story leads to another. . . . all the time it's connections, progress, meaning, this led to this, this happened because of this" (240). In the meantime, "readers of history" and "sufferers from history scan the pattern for hopeful conclusions, for the way ahead" (240).

Barnes' exploration of love, though at times poignant and touching, is for the most part shorn of sentimentality. Near the conclusion of "Parenthesis" Barnes proclaims that love "is our only hope even if it fails us, although it fails us, because it fails us" (243). Because of its vital connection with truth, love can stand as a sentinel against the invading armies of moral and epistemological relativism:

> Love and truth, yes that's the prime connection. We all know objective truth is not obtainable, that when some event occurs we shall have a multiplicity of subjective truths which we assess and then fabulate into history, into some 'God-

eyed' version of what 'really' happened. This God-eyed version is a fake—a charming, impossible fake. . . . But while we know this, we must still believe that objective truth is obtainable. . . . We must do so, because if we don't we're lost, we fall into beguiling relativity, we value one liar's version as much as another liar's. . . .

And so it is with love. We must believe in it or we're lost. We may not obtain it, or we may obtain it and find it renders us unhappy; we must still believe in it. If we don't then we merely surrender to the history of the world and to someone else's truth. (243-244)

X

A History of the World in 10 1/2 Chapters begins and ends with stories which are based on myths of death and resurrection. "The Stowaway," a somewhat irreverent retelling of the biblical Flood Myth, inaugurates a whole chain of narratives which center on disaster or failure (and in some cases with the human spirit's resilience in the face of these adversities). "The Dream," *A History*'s final chapter, reveals the tiny spark of "Odyssean" restlessnes in human nature which renders man unsuited for a life of eternal pleasure.

Like other stories in *A History* "The Dream" contains allusions to the narratives which precede it; in fact, a close reading of the story reveals that it functions as a kind of coda, in much the same way as Joyce's story "The Dead" recapitulates the major themes of *Dubliners*. Early in the story, for example, we learn that the narrator meets Noah ("The Dream" takes place in Heaven). Later, in a passage in which he talks about his appetite, the narrator reveals that he "ate more creatures than had ever sailed on Noah's Ark" (305). What is more, during one of his supermarket shopping sprees, the narrator purchases an alcoholic beverage called "Stinko-Paralytico," a name which recalls Charlie's description of his drunken stupor in "Upstream!" In still another section of the story, the speaker describes the building which he must report to to have his life "evaluated." According to his description, "There was marble everywhere and freshly polished brass and great stretches of mahogany that you knew would never get woodworm" (291). The old man who conducts the evaluation is kindly and avuncular—the complete antithesis of Noah in "The Stowaway." Finally, in the "coda" section of "The Dream," the narrator takes an inventory of all the things he has done while in Heaven. Many of the items he lists recall scenes and motifs from the earlier stories:

—I went on several cruises;
[recalling the cruises recounted throughout the book.]

—I learned canoeing, mountaineering, ballooning;
["canoeing" recalls "Upstream!", even though the vessels in that story are actually rafts; "mountaineering" recalls "The Mountain" and "Project Ararat."]
—I got into all sorts of danger and escaped;
[recalling the "Jonah" and "Titanic" narratives from "Three Simple Stories," as well as Franklin Hughes in "The Visitors" and the castaways in "Shipwreck."]
—I explored the jungle;
[again recalling "Upstream!"]
—I watched a court case (didn't agree with the verdict);
[a reference, perhaps, to the trial of the woodworm in "Wars of Religion."]
—I tried being a painter (not as bad as I thought!) and a surgeon;
[A reference which harks back to Gericault in "Shipwreck."]
—I fell in love, of course lots of time;
[echoing the loves of Franklin Hughes in "The Visitors" as well as the essay on love in "Parenthesis."]
—I pretended I was the last person on earth (and the first).
[in a sense, Noah was both of these.]

In "The Dream," Barnes ponders the blessings and paradoxes of Heaven. For the narrator, Heaven is initially (and "initially" apparently encompasses several millennia) an unending chain of sensual, gastronomic, and recreational delectations. On the surface everything is "perfect," including the narrator's breakfast grapefruit:

> Its flesh was pink for a start, not yellow, and each segment had already been carefully freed from its clinging membrane. The fruit itself was anchored to the dish by some prong or fork through its bottom, so that I didn't need to hold it or even touch it. I looked around for the sugar, but that was just out of habit. The taste seemed to come in two parts—a sort of awakening sharpness followed quickly by a wash of sweetness and each of those little globules . . . seemed to burst separately in my mouth. That was the grapefruit of my dreams, I don't mind telling you. (282)

In his "dream" only good things happen to the narrator. After devouring a savory breakfast, he finds a closet full of his favorite clothes, some of which had been discarded long ago by his wife. Later, he meets famous film stars and political figures, including Marilyn Monroe, John Wayne, Steve McQueen, Charlie Chaplin, John F. Kennedy, Dwight D. Eisenhower, Charles DeGaulle, Mao-Tse-Tung, and even Adolf Hitler (the narrator finds the "Fuhrer's" presence in Heaven baffling, to say the least). He reads that his favorite soccer team, which had never enjoyed a victory in championship play, has suddenly won a world cup. The narrator also marvels at his own newly acquired athletic abilities. For example, not long after checking into Heaven, he becomes a phenomenal golfer, shooting in the high sixties at first, but soon lowering those scores to an incredible eighteen—one stroke per hole! Afterwards, he masters soccer, cricket, and tennis (to the point where he actually begins beating some of the all-time great tennis stars). These sporting activities are punctuated by gargantuan shopping sprees, succulent repasts, and fantastic sexual encounters. The narrator soon discovers that in Heaven "You don't get tired—just kind of sated" (286). When tiredness does come, the narrator notes, it is a "sort of pleasant tiredness. Not one of those knackering tirednesses which just make you want to die" (297). Even prolonged indulgence of the senses leaves one with a feeling of being "pleasantly full," not glutted.

Moreover, the news is always good in Heaven.

> The newspapers were great. In a way it's the newspapers I remember best. Leicester City won the FA Cup, as I may have mentioned. They found a cure for cancer. My party won the General Election every single time until everyone saw its ideas were right and most of the opposition came over and joined us. Little old ladies got rich on the pools every week. Sex offenders repented and were released back into society and led blameless lives. Airline pilots learned how to save planes from mid-air collisions. Everyone got rid of nuclear weapons. . . . Children were innocent creatures once more; men and women were nice to one another; nobody's teeth had to be filled; and women's tights never laddered. (287–288)

But after several millennia, the narrator begins raising questions about Heaven—questions which reveal his growing uneasiness. For instance, he wants to know why he is being treated so well; what he owes in return; why he never had to take an "entrance exam" to enter Heaven; and why he has not met God yet. He broods over the implications of achieving perfection—over how, for instance, he will have used up golf after reaching the perfect score. After perfection, what is left? The narrator asks Margaret, his "Heavenly" attendant, if other "Heaveners" find all this perfection cloying? Margaret explains that ever since the establishment of the more hedonistic "New Heaven" most people become jaded by eternal pleasures. According to Margaret, "Old Heaven" was the place where people got what they deserved. In life, they had prayed, christened their children, and refrained from vulgar language and behavior. In Heaven, the "Old Heaveners," as Margaret refers to them, continue to live quiet lives devoted to prayer and worship. By contrast, "New Heaven" is run on completely different principles; it is more "democratic" than Old Heaven—which means that in New Heaven people get what they want, not what they deserve.

After a couple of millennia, however, the New Heaveners begin to get bored; in fact, some get so bored that they ask for pain and other "bad" things. Eventually they request another death. When the narrator complains that the idea of a second death jars with the whole conception of immortality and in effect cancels out the distinction between earthly life and heavenly life, Margaret replies:

> Yes, except don't forget the quality of life here is much better. People die when they decide they've had enough, not before. The second time round it's altogether more satisfying because it's willed. (303)

When the narrator asks about the types of people who tend to request death first, Margaret says:

> people who are a bit like you. People who want an eternity of sex, beer, drugs, fast cars—that sort of thing. They can't believe their good luck at first, and then, a few centuries later, they can't believe their bad luck. That is the sort of people they are. They're stuck with being themselves. Millennium after millennium of being themselves. (304)

The narrator then asks about the people who remain in Heaven the longest. Margaret replies that besides a few "tenacious" Old Heaveners, those with the greatest longevity are lawyers because "They love going over their old cases, and then going over everybody else's"; and scholars (here Barnes may be taking a swipe at literary critics), because

> 'They like sitting around reading all the books there are. And then they love arguing about them. Some of those arguments'—she cast an eye to the heavens—'go on for millennium after millennium. It just seems to keep them young, for some reason, arguing about books. (303)

The narrator later informs us that he too

> "took up reading. I remembered what Margaret said and tried—oh, for a few centuries or so—arguing about books with other people who'd read the same books. But it seemed a pretty arid life, at least compared to life itself" (306).

Chapter 4

The Porcupine

The subject of Barnes' most recent novel, *The Porcupine*, is the collapse of communism in Eastern Europe. Set in an unnamed European country, perhaps somewhere in the Balkans, *The Porcupine* evokes the mood of political distrust which permeates our world. On the surface of it, the book would seem to be a working out of what Peter Solinsky, one of the novel's main characters, describes as the legacy of Josef Stalin. Personifying the treachery, paranoia, and inhumanity which have distinguished 20th century world politics from that of all preceding ages, Stalin inaugurated the final stage of political man's descent into perfidy. According to Solinsky, when Stalin ordered the execution of his freind and political ally Sergei Kirov, he ushered in the "modern world":

> The assassination of Kirov. That was the key date. Stalin's friend and ally, Stalin's comrade. Therefore, as we innocently used to say, therefore the one person in the world who could not possibly have wished or hoped for it, let alone ordered it, was Stalin himself. This was an impossibility in all known political and personal terms. For Stalin to have ordered Kirov's death was not just 'out of character', but beyond our understanding of what character might comprise. . . . We have moved into an era when 'character' is a misleading concept. Character has been replaced by ego, and the exercise of authority as a reflection of power has been replaced by the psychopathic retention of power by all possible means, and in mockery of all implausibilities. Stalin had Kirov killed. Welcome to the modern world. (106)

The Porcupine's main plot, much of which is presented through the interior monologues of the novel's chief protagonists, revolves around the conflict between Stoyo Petkanov, the country's recently deposed communist leader who is on trial for crimes he committed while in power, and Peter Solinsky, the General Prosecutor who represents the new forces of democratization which are sweeping over Eastern Europe.

Despite appearances to the contrary, Solinsky, a former law professor under the communist regime, seems somewhat tentative in his new role as champion of the democratic ideals. This tentativeness may stem, in part, from the general mood of uncertainty which hangs over his country as it gropes toward democracy and a free-enterprise economy. But it may also derive from the frustration he experiences in his attempt to collect tangible evidence against Petkanov. What is more, just as his country is beset by all the problems attendant upon social and economic transformation, so Solinsky finds himself in the throes of a personal transition. As Robert Stone observes, in the newly appointed state prosecutor we witness a man who is "trying to believe in the ideals he professes, unwilling to face his own opportunism" (3). Though unquestionably Petkanov's intellectual equal, Solinsky—owing perhaps to his apprehensiveness—is often discountenanced by the ex-leader both in and out of court. When challenged about his motives for repudiating communism—first by Petkanov, who characterizes him as a traitor, and later by his own wife, who accuses him of being a self-righteous opportunist—Solinsky can only respond with hollow-sounding platitudes. In one scene, for instance, Petkanov—gloating over the new government's failure to provide adequate food, water, and electrical power for its people—reminds his adversary that during his regime comrades had both "sausage" and "higher things." To this, Solinsky replies:

> 'We give them freedom and truth.' It sounded pompous in his mouth, but it was what he believed, so why not state it? 'Freedom and truth!' replied Petkanov mockingly. 'So those are your higher things! You give the women the freedom to come out of their kitchens and march on your parliament and tell you this truth—that there is no fucking sausage in the shops. . . . And you call this progress?' (105)

Solinsky's concern about maintaining appearances also reflects his uneasiness with his new position. For instance, when he declines to move into the larger apartment which the new government offers him consequent to his appointment as state prosecutor, his wife becomes vexed. But as he explains his decision: "For the moment anyway: it hardly seemed tactful to accept any visible favour from the new government while charging its predecessor with massive abuse of privilege" (17).

Moreover, in his darker moods, Solinsky speculates on how history will treat Petkanov. If the prosecution succeeds in convicting the former President, will posterity then reverse the judgment of the court and vindicate him?

> Petkanov liked to boast that both his father and grandfather had lived to be centenarians. What would they do with him for the next twenty-five years? Peter had

a sudden, nauseating vision of the President's future rehabilitation. He saw a television series, *Stoyo Petkanov: My Life and Times*, starring a genial nonagenarian. He saw himself cast as a villain. (78)

And later Solinsky meditates on how

> Heroes become traitors, traitors become martyrs. Inspirational leaders and helmsmen of the nation become common criminals taken with their hands in the cashbox—until, perhaps, at some dread moment in the future, they become charming nonagenarians on TV chat shows. . . . Whether or not such revisionism occurred would partly depend on how he performed in the final week of the trial.
> And what did professors of law, prosecuting counsel, husbands, fathers become? What new names would be applied, what unnaming would take place? What chance for any of them in the breaking wave of history. (102–103)

Until recently, Solinsky had been a loyal member of the communist party. While growing up, young Peter had enjoyed the many privileges that came with being the son of a high-ranking party intellectual (who was later purged by Petkanov on the grounds that his intellect divorced him from the practical aspects of running a government). As a boy, Peter took pride in being a "Red Pioneer." He enjoyed accompanying his father to the party's annual political ceremonies, particularly those which commemorated the men and women who had perished in the Great Patriotic Struggle Against the Fascists. He was especially moved by the ceremonies that took place beneath "Alyosha," the enormous "Statue of Eternal Gratitude to the Liberating Red Army" which rose over the city like a great protector-god. The sight of this "heroic bronze soldier, left foot advancing steadfastly, head fixed nobly high, and higher still a brandished rifle with sparkling bayonet" (8), had stirred Peter's fledgling patriotic zeal: "Each year [Peter] believed more headily in solidarity between the socialist nations, in their progress, in their inevitable, scientific victory" (9). Even his father's sudden expulsion from the party had not shaken Peter's faith in the communist ideology: Peter "knew that the party was always greater than the individual, and that this applied in his father's case as in anyone else's" (26).

However, the recent deterioration of political conditions in his country had begun to erode Solinsky's devotion to the party. Moreover, he was becoming increasingly dissatisfied with his answers to the "innocent" questions that his daughter had been asking him about life in their country:

> Why were there so many soldiers when there wasn't any war? Why were there so many apricot trees in the countryside but never apricots in the shops? Why is there fog over the city in the summer? Why do all those people live on that waste ground beyond the eastern boulevards? The questions weren't dangerous and

> Peter had answered easily enough. Because they are there to protect us. Because we sell them abroad for hard currency that we need. Because there are many factories working at full capacity. Because gypsies choose to live that way.
>
> Angelina was always content with the answers. That was the shock. He hadn't been a father prodded into doubt by an innocent child's potent questions; what stirred him was the innocent child's passive satisfaction with responses he knew to be at best plausible evasions. (26–27)

The more Solinsky brooded over Angelina's "blithe acceptance" of his answers, the more he came to recognize it as a reflection of his country's intellectual and political inertia: "Angelina's condition expanded until it became symptomatic of the whole country. Could a nation lose its capacity for scepticism, for useful doubt? What if the muscle of contradiction simply atrophied from lack of exercise?" (27)

Solinsky's initial disaffection with communism was later fuelled by a local environmental issue that soon escalated into a major crisis for the party. It was the communists' inept handling of the problem which, in Solinsky's mind, undersocred the party's venality and ineffectiveness. Suddenly, the statue which had represented all that was good in the socialist world now loomed over the countryside like a gigantic symbol of the former government's tyranny. As State Prosecutor Solinsky gazes out at "Alyosha" from his apartment window, he thinks: "That's what has been stuck in the guts of my country for nearly fifty years. Now it was his job to help pull it down" (9).

Despite any misgivings he may secretly harbor, however, Solinsky looks forward to the role he will play in bringing Petkanov to justice—as much for personal as for political reasons:

> In prosecuting the former Head of State, Peter Solinsky was embarking on his most public form of self-definition. To newspaper columnists and TV commentators he represented the new order against the old, the future against the past, virtue against vice; and when he spoke to the media he customarily invoked the national conscience, moral duty, his plan of easing truth like a dandelion leaf from between the teeth of lies. (37)

From the outset, however, Solinsky's prosecution is hampered by the fact that he can charge Petkanov with only "minor" infractions. The crimes he would prefer to convict the former President of—defalcation of state funds, abrogation of freedom and human rights, and acts of state-sanctioned terrorism—prove too difficult to substantiate because of Petkanov's cleverness in concealing evidence. All potentially incriminating documents have either been shredded or misplaced, and the few extant records bear no signatures or fingerprints. Moreover, possible eyewitnesses to the alleged illegalities are either dead (most from "heart attacks") or missing. Thus, the only viable evidence which Solinsky can obtain is for offenses of a much less serious nature: abuse of privileges like the giving and receiving of gifts and special favors, private use of state vehicles, and exclusive access to the best food and clothing outlets for himself and other high ranking party officials. At one point, Solinsky even descends to accusing Petkanov of appropriating government fuel for private use. However, since the court tacitly views Petkanov as a scapegoat and his trial as a kind of symbolic exorcism, it really does not care how minor the accusations against the former leader are. It demands only that the prosecution acquire enough legitimate evidence to convict Petkanov of something, and that it conduct the proceedings in such a way as to ensure that the new government's already tarnished credibility will not suffer any further damage:

> In one respect, the trial was like most other trials that had taken place here over the previous forty years: the President of the Court, The Prosecutor General, the defense counsel and the accused—most of all the accused—knew that anything other than a verdict of guilty was unacceptable to higher authority. However, apart from this concluding certainty there were no fixed points, and no legal tradition to follow. . . . And although the actual charges were tightly drawn to minimize the possibility of the defendant evading conviction, The President of the Court and his two assessors felt an implied permission, bordering on a national duty, to let the proceedings sprawl.
>
> The Prosecutor General had similar powers to range widely in his cross-examinations and general speculations; all the bench had to do was ensure that this representative of the new government was not too obviously humiliated by the former President. (57–58)

Among those watching the nationally televised trial proceedings are Vera, Atanas, Dimiter, and Stefan—four young friends who had participated in the political demonstrations which eventually led to the downfall of Petkanov's government. Their observations, which Barnes strategically intersperses between Petkanov's courtroom statements, function as a kind of chorus. Counterpointing the fervent pro-democratic sentiments of the four young people is the staunch socialist outlook of Stefan's grandmother, a taciturn old woman who, fearing the changes taking place in her country, looks forward to the inevitable re-establishment of socialism. Among her most cherished possessions is an old framed portrait of Lenin.

As the trial gets under way, Vera insists that she will be content just to know the truth about the extent of Petkanov's crimes; however, her friends, who are not quite so easily placated, demand both the public humiliation and the execution of their former dictator:

> 'I hope they hang him,' said Dimiter the day before the trial began.
> 'Shoot him,' Atanas preferred. . . .
> 'I hope we learn the truth,' said Vera.
> 'I hope they just let him talk,' said Stefan. 'Just ask him simple questions to which there are simple answers, and then hear him come out with all that shit. How much did you steal? When did you order the murder of Simeon Popov? What is the number of your Swiss bank account? Ask him things like that, and watch how he doesn't answer a single one of them.' (23)

But Petkanov, who may be the "porcupine" of the title, proves to be a formidable opponent. Convinced that the new government has already determined his fate (ironically, of course, it has, making it no better than its predecessor), the combative former leader nevertheless stages an energetic defense, using the courtroom to grandstand his considerable rhetorical skills and to accost his accusers. When Solinsky accuses Petkanov of using his influence to illegally secure a spacious apartment for an actor who had been living in a dingy one-room flat, the former President bellows at the prosecutor, making his allegations look foolish and petty:

> What are these piddling charges? Who cares whether fifteen years ago some struggling actor was permitted to live in two rooms rather than one? If this is all you can find to accuse me of, then I cannot have done much wrong in thirty-three years as helmsman of this nation. (59–60)

Like Bernard Shaw's Undershaft, Petkanov is a master at unmasking the hypocrisies and pretensions of self-righteous people. He is confident that his adversaries will not do anything to make a martyr of him. A far more effective approach, he surmises, would be for the prosecution to attempt to discredit him, and this Petkanov will not permit to happen. He vehemently refuses to recognize the court's authority, arguing that he has been illegally arrested and detained. He succeeds in manipulating the media and turning the tables against his accusers by launching a volley of stunning counter-accusations. Though the perpetrator of unspeakable crimes against his countrymen, Petkanov argues that his successors are no less culpable than he. For example, when the prosecutor accuses the former leader of having misappropriated state funds, Petkanov is quick to remind Solinsky of the time when he (Solinsky), while in Italy on official state business, spent government money—money "provided for him by the sweat of the workers and the peasants at home"—not on "socialist books by our fraternal Italian colleagues, books worthy of study," or on donations to local orphanages, but rather on a new suit, an expensive dinner, and a prostitute.

During the trial, Petkanov seizes every opportunity to contrast the benefits which the country enjoyed while he was in power with the deplorable condition of the nation under the new regime:

> [People] want stability and hope. We gave them that. Things might not have been perfect, but with Socialism people could dream that someday they might be. You—you have only given them instability and hopelessness. A crime wave. The black market. Pornogarphy. Prostitution. Foolish women gibbering in front of priests again. The so-called Crown Prince offering himself as saviour of the nation. You are proud of these swift achievements? (69)

When Solinsky asserts that Petkanov had merely lied about the crime rate during his regime, the former President expresses his indignation over the fact that the new government condones the desecration of the memory of the First Leader (Petkanov's predecessor) by allowing pornogarphy to be sold on the steps of his mausoleum—to which the prosecutor, in one of his few successful counter-attacks, replies:

> You said you gave the people hope. No, what you gave them was fantasy. Big tits and huge cocks and everyone screwing one another endlessly, that's what your First Leader was selling, its political equivalent anyway. Your Socialism was just such a fantasy. More of one, in fact. At least there's some truth in what they're selling outside the Mausoleum nowadays. Some truth in that muck. (70)

Petkanov's numerous diatribes reveal both his intransigence and his keen political acumen. In one scene, for example, Solinsky contends that the former leader had in effect "raped" and "pillaged" the country by depositing large amounts of money in foreign banks. Petkanov quickly turns the argument around, insisting that it is his successors who are depredating the country by soliciting German and American investors. When the prosecutor counters by affirming that capitalist investment will have a salutary on the country's economy, Petkanov—who is not blind to the hidden evils of capitalistic imperialism—replies in such a way as to make the new government's solutions to social and economic problems seem naive and simplistic:

> 'Ha. They put a small amount of money into our country in order to take a larger amount out. That is the way of capitalism and imperialism, and those who allow it are not only traitors but economic cretins.' (60)

And when Solinsky talks proudly of the new freedoms which newspapers will enjoy under the present administration, Petkanov reminds him that the term "free newspaper" is a "contradiction. All newspapers belong to some party, some interest. Either the capitalists or the people. I'm surprised you haven't noticed" (41). Barnes' orchestration of the confrontations between these two antagonists seems to bear out what Maureen Howard has argued: "Barnes is aware that in staging his Shavian arguments he disarms us, prevents us from offering pat solutions to difficult problems" (137).

As Petkanov continues to distort the truth in order to make himself look innocent, guilt and accountability become lost in a maze of rationalizations and specious counter-arguments:

> Perfectly well-attested examples of the former President's colossal greed, his brazen acquisitiveness, his kleptomania and furious embezzling, just seemed to vanish in open court before the eyes of several million witnesses. The farm in the north-west province? A birthday present from the grateful nation on the twentieth anniversary of his appointment as Head of State, but in any case a gift only for his lifetime, and he rarely went there, and if he did it was only in order to entertain foreign dignitaries and thus advance the cause of Socialism and Communism. That house on the Black Sea? Offered him by the Writers' Union and the Lenin Publishing House for his services to literature. . . . That hunting lodge in the western hills? The Communist Party, in recognition of the fortieth anniversary . . . and so on, and so on. (66)

So as not to be completely outmaneuvered by his opponent, Solinsky—conscious of the fact that the defendant's mind "functions only to recall actions supposedly within the law" (108)—alludes to Petkanov's use of "selective memory" as a defense strategy:

> We have become more than familiar over the many weeks of this criminal case with your defense. Your defense to all charges and accusations. If something illegal was done, then you did not know about it. And if you did know about it, then automatically it was legal. (107–108)

The trial comes to a climax when Solinsky, frustrated by the former President's endless rhetorical prestidigitations, accuses Petkanov of the murder of his own daughter—the late Minister of Culture, Anna Petkanova. The accusation is based on a document that Solinsky received from head of security Lt. General Ganin. Dated 16 November 1971, this document, which bears only Petkanov's initials, authorized the use of "all necessary means" to combat counter-revolutionary activities. Apparently, several hard-line communists, having become suspicious of what they characterized as Anna Petkanova's growing "pro-Western" sympathies, had convinced the President to approve an order calling for her execution, lest she come to power after her father's death. What Solinsky hopes to establish based on the new evidence is that Anna's death was caused by the injection of a chemical poison which had the ability to simulate the symptoms of cardiac arrest. According to earlier records which Lt. General Ganin was able to produce, one of the former state departments—The Special Technical Branch of the Department of Internal Security—had been working on the development of just such a chemical during Petkanov's time in office and apparently with his knowledge. During his interrogation, Solinsky points out that this experimental drug was also linked to the deaths of two other political opponents: a broadcaster named Simeon Popov and a journalist named Miroslav Georgiev—both of whom had suffered fatal "heart attacks." On the basis of this evidence—evidence which Petkanov suspects has been forged—the ex-President is convicted and sentenced to thirty years of internal exile.

When the proceedings begin, Vera and her friends are confident that the trial will inaugurate a new era of freedom and truth:

> This was a great moment in their country's history, a farewell to grim childhood and grey, fretful adolescence. It was the end of lies and illusions; now the time had arrived when truth was possible, when maturity began. (20)

But as the trial wears on, the four friends become increasingly disenchanted and even cynical as they witness Petkanov making a mockery of justice. What the young people do not realize, however, is that Solinsky has also made a mockery of the proceedings by accepting falsified evidence from security chief Ganin. As he briefs Solinsky on this new piece of "evidence," Ganin—mindful that the trial is not going as well as had been expected owing both to the "trivial" nature of the charges against Petkanov and to the latter's resourcefulness in refuting them—intimates that the time has come to pursue a more vigorous prosecution:

> So what you must know—what, sir, you do know—is that the nation expects from this trial something more than a technical verdict of guilt on a charge of minor embezzlement. Which is the direction in which you are heading at the moment, with due respect. The nation expects to be shown that the defendant is the worst criminal in our entire history. This is your task. (94)

In his zeal to secure a major victory for the prosecution, Ganin had apparently drafted the executive order of 16 November 1971 himself and then forged Petkanov's initials on it. Meanwhile, intoxicated with his victory, Solinsky leaves the courthouse feeling that "he could take on anything" (111). But when he arrives home, his wife, Maria, berates him, calling him a "pimp" and characterizing his courtroom performance as "vulgar" and "worthy of American televsion" (110). Convinced that a man as clever as Petkanov would never have been so careless as to allow such damaging evidence to be found, Maria insinuates that her husband must have "bent the law" in order to convict the former leader. In a desperate attempt to salvage what little respect his wife has for him (as well as to shore up his own self-esteem), Solinsky resorts to some face-saving rationalizations:

> 'Peter, you don't really think that the worst criminal in our nation's history would sign such a useful document which Ganin just happened to discover when the prosecution wasn't having the success he'd hoped?'
> Naturally, he had considered that, and was ready with his defenses. If Petkanov hadn't signed that memorandum, he must have signed something like it. We are only putting into concrete form an order he must have given over the telephone. Or with a handshake, a nod, a pertinent failure to disapprove. The document is true, even if it is a forgery. Even if it isn't true, it is necessary. Each excuse was weaker, yet also more brutal. (113)

Just as she had been threatening to do for some time, Maria takes Angelina and leaves home. Her husband, beleaguered by his long battle with Petkanov and now agitated by Maria's estrangement, takes a taxi to the site of the Statue of Eternal Gratitude—which is soon to be torn down and stored in the city's scrap heap beside the dismantled icons of other fallen communist leaders. Asked by Solinsky how he feels about the imminent demolition of "Alyosha," the cab driver, freighting his words "with obvious irony," replies, "Comrade Chief, now that we're all free and can speak our minds, permit me to inform you that I don't give a fuck either way" (128)—a comment which not only reflects the growing indifference of the general populace but also prefigures the novel's ambiguous conclusion.

This ambiguity may derive from Barnes' distrust of ideological block theories, like "capitalism," "democracy," and "communism." On the one hand, the demise of Petkanov's socialist government and the signs of approaching spring hold out the possibility that democracy will take root and that Solinsky will survive his personal crises. From the great public gardens which spread out beneath the statue,

> Peter Solinsky looked down over the bare chestnuts and walnuts, all weeks away from leaf . . . . To the south lay the smogbound city, guarded by its domestic ramparts. . . . Perhaps he should get a new place to live, as Maria had suggested. . . . Just because Maria wasn't coming, it didn't mean he had to live in a dingy mouse-hole. Six rooms, perhaps? A prosecutor general sometimes has to receive dignitaries at home. And then, well, he wouldn't be divorced forever. (128)

Just before leaving the gardens, Solinsky places two woolen tassels, called *martenitsas*, under a large stone. According to local superstition, the *martenitsas* drive away evil spirits and bring good luck and health:

> A few days later you would go to where you had left the *Martenitsas*. If there were ants under the stone, there would be lambs on the farm that year; worms and bugs meant horses and cattle; spiders stood for donkeys. Any living thing that stirred promised you fertility, a new beginning. (129)

But the democracy which replaces Petkanov's government is itself deeply flawed, as is attested not only by Solinsky's expediential use of "unlawful" evidence to convict Petkanov but also by the new government's failure to improve its citizens' quality of life. As Robert Stone argues: "the work of Julian Barnes has often thrived on various levels of irony, on the reduction and dissection of illusion" (44). For the average people of Barnes' fictional East European country, genuine democratic reform is merely a mirage; to them, the only things which have changed are the names of the various government bureaucracies ("The Department of Internal Security" becomes "The Patriotic Security Forces"; "The Office of State Security" becomes "The Ministry of Justice").

Though somewhat "traditional" in style and narrative form, *The Porcupine* nevertheless exemplifies several important tendencies in postmodernist fiction. For one thing, *The Porcupine* reveals postmodernism's antipathy toward the great ideological "metanarratives" which have dominated human experience for so many centuries. In this fictional account of the recent "democratic" revolution in Russia and Eastern Europe, a totalitarian socialist government is supplanted by an inept democracy whose bureaucratic machinery is as sluggish as its predecessor's was ruthless.

Moreover, the novel's seeming "journalistic" verisimilitude is occasionally undermined by elements which call attention to the text's fictiveness. These elements include not only the "interior monologues," or "soliloquies," of the main characters, which disrupt the primary narrative diegesis, but also the occasional eradication of spatial distances. As we saw earlier, the statements which Petkanov makes during his hearings are interspersed with the comments of four young people who are not actually present in the courtroom, but rather in their apartments, where they are watching the trial on television. Adding to the fictive artificiality of these scenes is the use of italics to record the viewers' remarks:

> 'I am an ordinary man. I need little. I have never, during all my years as helmsman, asked much for myself.'

> ['*The fool asks much, but he is more of a fool who grants it.*']
> 'I have simple tastes. I do not require many things.'
> ['*What can you need when you own the whole country. Us too. Us.*']
> 'I have no money hoarded away in Switzerland.'
> ['*It must be somewhere else then.*']
> 'When they found gold on my land, I gave it voluntarily to the National Archeaological Museum.'
> ['*He prefers silver.*']
> 'I am not like the imperialist presidents of the United States, who present themselves to their fellow-countrymen as simple folk, and then leave office laden with riches.'
> ['*Us, us!*']
> '. . . When the Lenin Publishing House insisted that I took royalties on my books . . . I always gave half away to the orphanages. This was not always publicised.'
> ['*We are the orphans.*']
> 'My late wife never dressed in Paris fashions.'
> ['*She should have. Bag of suet. Raisa! Raisa!*'] (83–84)

Ironically, another device which calls attention to the novel's fictiveness is the use of historical figures. For example, in one of his "soliloquies" at the beginning of the novel, Petkanov assails Russia's Mikhail Gorbachev for consorting with American capitalists and their culture-idols. According to Petkanov, it was the Soviet President who had proclaimed that the "Brezhnev Doctrine" would soon give way to the "Sinatra Doctrine":

> The Sinatra Doctrine. Toadying to Uncle Sam like that. And who was Sinatra? Some Italian in a shiny suit who went around with the mafia all the time. Someone Nancy Reagan went down on her knees to. Yes, that made sense. It all started with Frank Sinatra, the whole fucking thing. Sinatra fucked Nancy Reagan in the White House, that's what they said, didn't they? Reagan couldn't control his wife. And Gorbachev couldn't control his wife. And Gorbachev's spokesman says we're all going to follow the Frank Sinatra Doctrine. The Elvis Presley Doctrine. The McDonald's Hamburger Doctrine. The Doctrine of Mickey Mouse and Donald Duck. (18–19)

Petkanov then remembers reading a KGB document in which it was reported that American Presidents feel most safe at Disneyland because no assassin would dare to strike there: "It would be sacrilege, it would be an offence against the great gods of Mickey Mouse and Donald Duck" (19).

In another scene which contains a reference to an historical figure, Petkanov compares his arrest with that of Jean-Bedel Bokassa, the emperor of The Central African Republic who was imprisoned in 1986 for embezzlement, murder, and cannibalism. Just before the trial begins,

Petkanov reminds his accusers that if found guilty, he will join Bokassa as the only other head of state in modern history to be tried for and convicted of political crimes. Later, as he ponders his own fate, Petkanov laments the execution of Nicolae Ceausescus, a leader whom he claims to have embraced on numerous occasions:

> Nicolae. They shot him. On Christmas Day, too. Yes, but in hot blood, chased him from his palace, followed his helicopter, trailed his car, dragged him out before what they laughably called a people's court, found him guilty of murdering 60,000 people, shot him, shot them both, Nicolae and Elena, just like that. . . . (17)

Shortly afterwards, Petkanov, brimming with pride, recalls the day when China's Mao-Tse-Tung praised him for his unswerving loyalty to the Communist Party and his untiring leadership. And near the end of his trial, the former President reads excerpts from statements by various heads of state commending him for his outstanding qualifications and his achievements as a political leader. The list of contributors includes Queen Elizabeth II, Prime Minister Margaret Thatcher, Presidents Nixon and Carter, Andreas Popandreou of Greece, King Juan Carlos of Spain, France's Valery Giscard d'Estaing, UN Secretary General Javier Perez de Cuellaer, and Egyptian President Hosni Mubarak.

Barnes' use of real-world figures like Frank Sinatra, Mikhail Gorbachev, and "that fascist Yeltsin" not only authenticates the "historical context" which his novel projects but also foregrounds the ontological boundaries between fiction and reality. Barnes himself reveals his awareness of the fiction/reality ontology. In an essay entitled "Stranger Than Fiction," which he wrote for *The New Yorker* in October of 1992, Barnes intimates that his portrayal of Stoyo Petkanov was based, in part, on Bulgaria's Todor Zhivkov, who in September of 1991 became the first former Communist leader in Eastern Europe to be imprisoned. After admitting that he had used an "outline of the Zhivkov trial (plus various specifics)" for his plot, Barnes puzzles over the Bulgarians' reception of the book: would "they think I had imaginatively transformed their recent history or pillaged and perverted it? Would they even view the book as a novel, rather than just history à clef?" And in another comment which reveals postmodernist fiction's preoccupation with the relation of art to life, Barnes observes: "There were certainly problems over the demarcation line between fiction and reality. Some [Bulgarians] complained that my dictator was more intelligent than theirs had been; others wanted to correct what they saw as factual errors."

According to Brian McHale, the intrusion of historical figures into fictional texts

> has the scent of scandal about it. And what, exactly, is the source of the scandal? Ultimately, its source is ontological: boundaries between worlds have been violated. There is an ontological scandal when a real world figure is inserted in a fictional situation,where he interacts with purely fictional characters. (85)

Moreover, unlike writers of traditional historical fiction, contemporary historical fictionists often employ what McHale refers to as "transworld" figures in order to achieve parodic or satirical effects. For example, in the wild "mock-auction" scene in *The Porcupine*—a scene which recalls (and enacts) Bakhtin's notion of the "Carnival"—Petkanov's blanket, which his housekeeper had earlier testified was his only earthly possession, is sold off—along with his genitals and a pair of his sandals—to such bidders as Saddam Hussein, George Bush, Emperor Bokassa, Mahatma Gandhi, Josef Stalin, and "several claimants of both sexes purporting to be Stoyo Petkanov's secret lover" (97).

However, the most overt intersection of the fictional and the historical in *The Porcupine* is the relationship between Petkanov and Mikhail Gorbachev. The fact that these two figures inhabit totally disparate ontological worlds does not prevent Petkanov from recalling specific conversations that he had with the Soviet leader. In one conference Petkanov proposes a union between his country and Russia. But Gorbachev, suspicious that his "comrade" is using this as a ploy to evade payment of his country's debts, rejects the idea. From that point on, their relationship deteriorates. Referring to him as "that weak fool in the Kremlin who looked as if a bird had shat on his head" and "that cunt in the Kremlin," Petkanov denounces Gorbachev for betraying communism and selling out to the West.

Though Barnes' primary motive for introducing historical figures into his novel may be to achieve a kind of documentary verisimilitude—a device used in many conventional historical fictions—it is also possible that he is attempting to exploit the kinds of effects which postmodernist historical fictions have achieved—the interpenetration of different ontological dimensions to foreground and thematize the relationship between fiction and reality. Thus, *The Porcupine* both engages contemporary historical reality and insists on maintaining its status as a work of fiction—a juxtaposition which Andreas Huyssen argues is central to the postmodernist literary experience. In his *After the Great Divide*, Huyssen speaks of the need to abandon that dead-end dichotomy of politics and aesthetics which for too long has dominated accounts of modernism, including the aesthetic trend within poststructuralism. The point is not to eliminate the productive tension between the political and the aesthetic, between history and the text, between engagement and the mission of art. The point is to heighten that tension, even to rediscover it and bring it back into the arts as well as in criticism. (221)

Bibliography

Abbas, M.A. "Photography/Writing/Postmodernism." *Minnesota Review* 23 (1984): 1–22.

Alexander, Marguerite. *Flights From Realism: Themes and Strategies in Postmodernist British and American Fiction*. London: Edward Arnold, 1990.

Alter, Robert. *Partial Magic: The Novel as Self-Conscious Genre*. Berkeley: University of California Press, 1975.

Bakhtin, Mikhail. *The Dialogic Imagination*. Trans. Caryl Emerson andMichael Holquist. Ed. Michael Holquist. Austin: University of Texas Press, 1981.

Barnes, Julian. *Metroland*. New York: McGraw-Hill, 1980.

———. *Before She Met Me*. New York: McGraw-Hill, 1982.

———. *Flaubert's Parrot*. New York: McGraw-Hill, 1984.

———. *A History of the World in 10 1/2 Chapters*. New York: Vintage Books, 1989.

———. *Talking It Over*. New York: Alfred A. Knopf, 1991.

———. *The Porcupine*. New York: Alfred A. Knopf, 1992.

Barth, John. "The Literature of Exhaustion." *Atlantic* 2 (1967): 29–34.

———. "The Literature of Replenishment.' *Atlantic* 1 (1980): 65–71.

Bayley, John. "Time of Indifference." Rev of *The Porcupine* by Julian Barnes. *The New York Review* 17 Dec. 1992.

Belsey, Catherine. *Critical Practice*. London: Methuen, 1980.

Behabib, Seyla. "Epistemologies of Postmodernism: A Rejoinder to Jean-Francois Lyotard." *New German Critique* 33 (1984): 103-26.

Bennett, David. "Wrapping Up Postmodernism: The Subject of Consumption Versus the Subject of Cognition." *Textual Practice* 3 (1987); 243-61.

Bradbury, Malcolm. Introduction. *Newwriting.* Ed. Malcolm Bradbury and Judy Cooke. London: Minerva, 1992. 1-10.

Brombert, Victor. *The Novels of Flaubert: A Study of Themes and Techniques.* Princeton: Princeton University Press, 1966.

Calinescu, Matei and Douwe Fokkema, eds. *Exploring Postmodernism.* Philadelphia: John Benjamins, 1987.

Chow, Rey. "Rereading Mandarin Ducks and Butterflies: A Response to the 'Postmodern' Condition." *Cultural Critique* 5 (1987): 69-93.

Collins, James. "Postmodernism and Cultural Practice: Redefining the Parameters." *Postmodern Screen* issue of *Screen 2* (1987): 47-67.

Coward, David. "The Rare Creature's Human Sounds." Rev. of *Flaubert's Parrot* by Julian Barnes. *Times Literary Supplement* 5 Oct 1984: 1117-1118.

Culler, Jonathan. *Flaubert: The Uses of Uncertainty.* Ithaca: Cornell University Press, 1974.

"Culture and Consciousness: The Twentieth-Century English Novel." *Prentice Hall Guide to English Literature.* Ed. Marion Wynne-Davies. New York: Prentice Hall, 1990.

Daiches, David. *The Novel and the Modern World.* Chicago: University of Chicago Press, 1960.

Davis, Mike. "Urban Renaissance and the Spirit of Postmodernism." *New Left Review* 151 (1985): 106-113.

De Man, Paul. *Allegories of Reading: Figural Language in Rousseau, Nietzsche, Rilke, and Proust.* New Haven: Yale University Press, 1979.

D'Haen, Theo. *Text to Reader: A Communicative Approach to Fowles, Barth, Cortazar, and Boon.* Philadelphia: John Benjamins, 1983.

Dipple, Elizabeth. *The Unresolvable Plot.* London: Routledge, 1988.

During, Simon. "Postmodernism or Post-Colonialism Today." *Textual Practice* 1 (1987): 32–47.

Eagleton, Terry. *Literary Theory: An Introduction.* Minneapolis: University of Minnesota Press, 1983.

———. *Criticism and Ideology: A Study in Marxist Literary Theory.* Norfolk: Thetford Press Limited, 1975.

———. "Capitalism, Marxism and Postmodernism." *New Left Review* 152 (1985): 60–73.

Federman, Raymond, ed. *Surfiction: Fiction Now and Tomorrow.* Chicago: Swallow Press, 1981.

Fokkema, Douwe and Elrud Ibsch. *Theories of Literature in the Twentieth Century.* New York: St. Martin's Press, 1978.

Foley, Barbara. *Telling the Truth: The Theory and Practices of Documentary Fiction.* Ithaca: Cornell University Press, 1986.

Forster, E.M. *Aspects of the Novel.* London: Edward Arnold, 1927.

Forster, Hal, ed. *The Anti-Aesthetic: Essays on Postmodern Culture.* Port Townsend, Wash.: Bay Press, 1983.

Garvin, Harry. *Romanticism, Modernism and Postmodernism.* Lewisburg: Bucknell University Press, 1980.

Genies, Bernard. "Un Anglais Flaubert et les perroquets." *La Quinzaine Litteraire* (April 1986): 24–27.

Genette, Gerard. *Narrative Discourse: An Essay in Method.* Trans. Jane Lewin. Ithaca: Cornell University Press, 1980.

Giddens, Anthony. "Modernism and Postmodernism." *New German Critique* 22 (1981): 15–18.

Gindin, James. *Postwar British Fiction: New Accents and Attitudes.* Berkeley: University of California Press, 1963.

Graff, Gerard. *Literature Against Itself: Literary Ideas in Modern Society.* Chicago: University of Chicago Press, 1979.

Greenberg, Clement. "Modern and Postmodern." *Arts Magazine* 6 (1980): 64–66.

Hassan, Ihab. *The Postmodern Turn: Essays in Postmodern Theory and Culture.* Columbus: Ohio State University Press, 1987.

Hayman, David. "Double-Distancing: An Attribute of the 'Postmodern' Avant-Garde." *Novel* 1 (1978): 33–47.

Higdon, David. "'Unconfessed Confessions': The Narrators of Graham Swift and Julian Barnes." *The British and Irish Novel Since 1960.* Ed. James Acheson. New York: St. Martin's Press, 1991. 174–191.

Higdon, David. *Shadows of the Past in Contemporary British Fiction.* Athens: University of Georgia Press, 1985.

Hoffman, Gerhard. "'Modern,' 'Postmodern,' and 'Contemporary', as Criteria for the Analysis of Twentieth Century Literature." *Amerikastudien* 22 (1977): 19–46.

Howard, Maureen. "Barnes' *The Porcupine.*" *The Yale Review* 81 (1993): 134–137.

Howe, Irving. "The Idea of the Modern." *Irving Howe: Selected Writings 1950–1990.* Ed. Irving Howe. New York: Harcourt Brace Jovanovich, 1990.

Hutcheon, Linda. *Narcissistic Narrative: The Metafictional Paradox.* Ontario: Wilfrid Laurier University Press, 1980.

———. *A Poetics of Postmodernism: History, Theory, Fiction.* London: Routledge, 1988.

———. *A Theory of Parody: The Teachings of Twentieth Century Art Forms.* London, Methuen, 1985.

———. *The Politicis of Postmodernism.* London: Routledge, 1989.

Huyssen, Andreas. *After the Great Divide: Modernism, Mass Culture, Postmodernism.* Indianapolis: Indiana University Press, 1986.

Jameson, Frederic. *The Political Unconscious: Narrative as a Socially Symbolic Act.* Ithaca: Cornell University Press, 1981.

Josipovici, Gabriel. *The World and the Book.* London: Macmillan, 1971.

Karl, Frederick. *A Reader's Guide to the Contemporary English Novel.* New York: Farrar, Straus and Giroux, 1972.

Korg, Jacob. Introduction. *Twentieth Century Interpretations of Bleak House*. Englewood Cliffs: Prentice Hall, 1968.

Kramer, Hilton. "Postmodern Art and Culture in the 1980s." *New Criterion* 1 (1982): 36–42.

Laffey, John. "Cacophonic Rites: Modernism and Postmodernism." *Historical Reflections* 1 (1987): 1–32.

Langbaum, Robert. *The Modern Spirit*. London: Oxford University Press, 1970.

Latimer, Dan. "Jameson and Postmodernism. *New Left Review* 148 (1984): 116–27.

Leavis, F.R. *The Great Tradition*. New York: New York University Press, 1960.

Lee, Alison. *Realism and Power: Postmodern British Fiction*. London: Routledge, 1990.

Lehman, David. "From Death to Birth." Rev. of *Time's Arrow* by Martin Amis. *The New York Times Book Review* 17 Nov. 1991: 15.

Levenson, Michael. "Flaubert's Parrot." Rev. of *Talking It Over* by

Julian Barnes. *The New Republic* 205 16 Dec. 1991: 42–44.

Levin, Harry. *The Gates of Horn: A Study of Five French Realists*. New York: Oxford University Press, 1966.

Lodge, David. *The Novelist at the Crossroads and Other Essays on Fiction and Criticism*. London: ARK Paperbacks, 1986.

———. *After Bakhtin: Essays on Fiction and Criticism*. London: Routledge, 1990.

———. "The Novelist Today: Still at the Crossroads?" *Newwriting*. Ed. Malcolm Bradbury and Judy Cooke. London: Minerva, 1992. 203–215.

Lukacs, Georg. *The Theory of the Novel*. Trans. Anna Bostock. Cambridge: The MIT Press, 1971.

———. *The Historical Novel*. Lincoln: University of Nebraska Press, 1962.

Lyotard, Jean-Francois. *The Postmodern Condition: A Report on Knowledge.* Trans Geoff Bennington and Brian Massumi. Minneapolis: University of Minnesota Press, 1984.

McGrath, Patrick. "Julian Barnes." *Bomb* 21 (Fall 1987): 20–23.

McHale, Brian. *Postmodernist Fiction.* London: Routledge, 1992.

Malmgren, Carl Daryll. "'From Work to Text,' The Modernist and Postmodernist Kunstlerroman." *Novel* 1 (1985): 5–28.

Marshall, Brenda. *Teaching the Postmodern: Fiction and Theory.* London: Routledge, 1992.

Massie, Allan. *The British Novel Today 1970–1989.* London: Longman, 1990.

Menand, Louis. *Discovering Modernism: T.S. Eliot and His Context.* New York: Oxford University Press, 1987.

Millington, Mark and Alison Sinclair. "The Honourable Cuckold: Models of Masculine Defense." *Comparative Literature Studies* 29 (1992): 1–19.

Nadeau, Maurice. *The Greatness of Flaubert.* Trans. Barbara Bray. La-Salle, Illinois: Open Court Publishing Company, 1972.

Nagele, Rainer. "Modernism and Postmodernism: The Margins of Articulation." *Studies in Twentieth Century Literature* 5 (1981): 5–25.

Newman, Charles. *The Post-Modern Aura: The Act of Fiction in an Age of Inflation.* Evanston: Northwestern University Press, 1985.

Norris, Christopher. *What's Wrong With Postmodernism?: Critical Theory and the Ends of Philosophy.* Baltimore: The John Hopkins University Press, 1990.

Palmer, Richard. "Postmodernity and Hermeneutics." *boundary* 2 (1977): 363–93.

Raulet, Gerard. "From Modernity as One-Way Street to Postmodernity as Dead End." *New German Critique* 33 (1984): 155–177.

Salgas, Jean-Pierre. "Julian Barnes n'en a pas fini avec Flaubert." *La Quinzaine Litteraire* (May 1986): 16–31.

Scherpe, Klaus. "Dramatization and De-Dramatization of 'the end': The Apocalyptic Consciousness of Modernity and Postmodernity." *Cultural Critique* 5 (1986/7): 95–127.

Scholes, Robert. *Fabulation and Metafiction*. Urbana: University of Illinois Press, 1979.

Sinfield, Alan. *Literature, Politics, and Culture in Postwar Britain*. Berkeley: University of California Press, 1989.

Spanos, William. *Repetitions: The Postmodern Occasion in Literature and Culture*. Baton Rouge: Louisiana State University Press, 1987.

Stam, Robert. *Reflexivity in Film and Literature From Don Quixote to Jean-Luc Godard*. Ann Arbor: UMI Research Press, 1985.

Stephenson, Andres. "Regarding Postmodernism—A Conversation with Frederic Jameson." *Social Text* 17 (1987): 29–54.

Stone, Robert. "A Cold Peace." Rev. of *The Porcupine* by Julian Barnes. *The New York Times Book Review* 13 Dec. 1992: 3.

Sturrock, John. *The French New Novel: Claude Simon, Michel Butor, and Alain Robbe-Grillet*. New York: Oxford University Press, 1969.

Tanner, Tony. *City of Words: American Fiction 1950–1970*. New York: Harper and Row, 1971.

Thiher, Allen. *Words in Reflection: Modern Language Theory and Postmodern Fiction*. Chicago: University of Chicago Press, 1984.

Todd, Richard. "Confrontation Within Convention: On The Character Of British Postmodernist Fiction." *Postmodern Fiction in Europe and the Americas*. Ed. Theo D'haen and Hans Bertens. Amsterdam: Rodopi, 1988. 115–125.

Vargas Llosa, Mario. *The Pertpetual Orgy: Flaubert and Madame Bovary*. Trans. Helen Lane. New York: Farrar, Straus, and Giroux, 1984.

Waugh, Patricia. *Metafiction: The Theory and Practice of Self-Conscious Fiction*. London: Routledge, 1984.

White, Hayden. *Tropics of Discourse: Essays in Cultural Criticism*. Baltimore: The John Hopkins University Press, 1978.

White, Patti. *Gatsby's Party: The System and the List in Contemporary Narrative.* Indiana: Purdue University Press, 1992.

Wilde, Alan. *Horizons of Assent: Modernism, Postmodernism, and the Ironic Imagination.* Baltimore: John Hopkins University Press, 1981.

Wilson, Edmund. *Axel's Castle.* New York: Charles Scribner's Sons, 1931.

Wood, Michael. "In Search of Love and Judgment." Rev. of *A History of the World in 10 1/2 Chapters* by Julian Barnes. *Times Literary Supplement* 30 June–6 July 1989: 713–715.